From Nighthawk to Spitfire

From Nighthawk to
Spitfire
The Aircraft of
R.J. Mitchell

JOHN K. SHELTON

The
History
Press

Back cover image: Mitchell (third from right) and supermarine workers with the tools of their trade, courtesy of P. Jarrett.

First published 2015

The History Press
The Mill, Brimscombe Port
Stroud, Gloucestershire, GL5 2QG
www.thehistorypress.co.uk

British Library Cataloguing in Publication Data.
A catalogue record for this book is available from the British Library.

ISBN 978 0 7509 6222 3

Typesetting and origination by The History Press
Printed and bound in Malta by Melita Press

CONTENTS

1

THE MAN

NO FLASH IN THE PAN

One has only to reflect for a moment on the remarkable advent and success of the Spitfire to realise that R.J. Mitchell's fighter must surely have resulted from considerable previous experience of high speed flight. It is not just air enthusiasts who might still remember his designs, which won the international Schneider Trophy four times, contributing most significantly to the design of the famous fighter.

However, as we shall see, most of Mitchell's aeronautical experience was with much slower seaplanes or with even slower amphibians, and it was by no means predictable that he would go on to produce the iconic fighter so strongly associated in the popular mind with the Battle of Britain. Indeed, the designer of this wide range of aircraft types – from transport or reconnaissance seaplanes to high speed Trophy racers – started out in locomotive engineering and never had any formal education as an aircraft designer.

Yet, well before the Spitfire appeared, he had emerged as one of the most prominent designers of his time, and a listing of his most significant contributions to aviation reveals promise from the very beginning:

The Commercial Amphibian, his first independent design, won an enhanced award at the 1920 Air Ministry competition for passenger amphibian flying boats. Although this aircraft came second to the Vickers Viking, because of the lower powered engine provided by his company, the second prize of £4,000 was doubled in recognition of the promise that the aircraft had shown.

His modification and uprating of an earlier company machine, the Sea Lion II, won the Schneider Trophy competition for Britain in 1922.

ABOVE: 'I have seen the future, and it works.' – Lincoln Steffens. R.J. Mitchell (right) with his S6 Schneider Trophy winner. (Courtesy of Solent Sky Museum)
PREVIOUS: R.J. Mitchell (c.1930). (Courtesy of Solent Sky Museum)

The small fleet of his Sea Eagle flying boats formed the first British scheduled flying boat service, operating between Southampton and the Channel Islands 1923–1928.

His Swan of 1924, a larger scale development of the Commercial Amphibian which joined the Sea Eagle fleet, was claimed by Supermarine to be the world's first multi-engined, amphibian passenger-carrying machine.

The above mentioned flying boat service was incorporated into the newly formed Imperial Airways Ltd (later British Airways) in 1924.

His Scarab, also in 1924, equipped the Royal Spanish Air Force with a fleet of twelve military aircraft, and for its time, represented a formidable amphibious bomber gunship. This order represented a significant step towards establishing Supermarine as a prosperous aircraft company.

His Southampton flying boat, a military development of the Swan, was ordered, unusually in 1925, straight off the drawing board and became the standard RAF coastal reconnaissance aircraft, replacing less satisfactory machines of First World War design. A total of twenty-four Mark Is were built, and this established real stability and prosperity for Supermarine. Pilots reported that they were trouble free and 'a joy to fly', and *Jane's* described the design as 'one of the most notable successes in post-war design'. Additionally, it was described as 'probably the most beautiful biplane flying boat that had ever been built' and its trendsetting upswept rear hull attracted the comment that it had 'certainly the most beautiful hull ever built'.

In the same year, Mitchell also produced his S4 Schneider Trophy racer, which revolutionised the design of virtually all successive competition entries. He moved, in one bold step, from the usual wire-braced biplanes to a startlingly new cantilever monoplane. Compared with the top speed of 175mph claimed for his Sea Lion in 1923, the S4 gained the world speed record for seaplanes and the outright British speed record for all types, with 226.75mph only two years later.

In 1926 Mitchell appointed one of the first metallurgists to the aircraft industry, which had previously worked almost exclusively with wooden airframes, and his metal-hulled Southampton Mark II was in the forefront of the movement towards all-metal aircraft construction. A total of seventy-nine metal-hulled machines were produced, as well as numerous hulls for retrofitting to the wooden-hulled Mark I, even further enhancing the prosperity and status of Supermarine.

The increased efficiency of the Mark II Southampton led to the RAF being equipped for a special Far East Flight of four of these machines. The aircraft completed a 27,000 mile cruise between October 1927 and February 1928 to Singapore, and then around Australia, which had only been visited by aircraft on four previous occasions and only circumnavigated by one earlier machine. The sixty-two timetabled stages were completed by all the aircraft. The Supermarine publicity said, '108,000 machine miles, giving no trouble of any consequence', and as the *Daily Mail* said, 'the flight will rank as one of the greatest feats in the history of aviation'.

In 1930, Supermarine were awarded a contract (later cancelled by the government) to build the largest wingspan flying boat in the world – greater than the famous Dornier Do X, and only to be surpassed by the Hughes H-4 Hercules of 1947.

By this time, Mitchell had designed his next two Schneider Trophy racers, the S5 and S6, which respectively won the 1927 and 1929 contests. In the following event of 1931, his uprated S6B won the trophy outright and later went on to set a new absolute air speed record of 407.5mph. This last machine was now made entirely of metal, stressed-skin construction and clearly looked towards the Spitfire, five years later.

In 1934, the last of his medium-sized amphibians, the Walrus, was ordered by the Royal Australian Air Force and, in the following year, by the Royal Air Force. Eventually a total of 746 were built. It became the standard naval fleet spotter and provided the British armed forces with their slowest aircraft, with its fastest (the Spitfire) soon to follow.

At the age of 36, Mitchell was described in Supermarine publicity as, 'One of the leading flying boat, amphibian and high speed seaplane designers in the country.' He had also been invited to give a talk on the BBC, had been elected a Fellow of the Royal Aeronautical Society and awarded the CBE.

The above successes, which were achieved before his early death at the age of 42, clearly suggested that he might well be entrusted with the design of an outstanding fighter when the need arose, but it was especially fortunate that he had become involved with the design of the later Schneider Trophy machines, as these

Reginald Joseph Mitchell CBE in the garden of his house, Portswood, Southampton, 1931. (Courtesy of Solent Sky Museum)

gave him unfettered opportunities to extend the boundaries of high speed flight. As a result, the advent of the Spitfire prototype of 1936 marked a dramatic increase of more than 100mph over the most recent RAF fighter in service, and led to an even more dramatic and unprecedented initial order of 310, three months after its first service trial.

He died, however, without seeing the fighter go into squadron service and without knowing that nearly 23,000 examples were to be built, in a multitude of variants.

In the pages which follow, the progressive stages in the remarkable career of R.J. Mitchell will be described. But first it will appropriate to describe something of the character and capacity for hard work that produced these significant landmarks.

R.J. MITCHELL'S WORK ETHIC

The earlier listing of Mitchell's successes (and there were also some failures) indicates a considerable output in his relatively short working life, and this is obviously not simply attributable to talent. A capacity for hard, concentrated work was also clearly involved, especially when one comes to consider the variety of aircraft he was called upon to design.

For example, between 1920 and 1922, the newly appointed chief designer, with only three previous years' experience in the aircraft industry, was responsible for the design of a passenger-carrying prototype (the Commercial Amphibian) which required the innovation of a retracting undercarriage design; a fleet spotter (the Seal) with the added complexity of folding wings; beginning the design for a replacement for the large First World War Felixstowe coastal reconnaissance flying boat (the Scylla); and the modification of an earlier company machine for the 1922 Schneider Trophy contest (the Sea Lion II).

This varied output, which was extended to land planes in 1924 with the Sparrow, was described by Arthur Black, Mitchell's chief metallurgist, as follows:

> In the sixteen years after he became chief designer at the age of 24, he designed the incredible number [of twenty-five machines] ranging from large flying boats and amphibians to light aircraft, and from racing planes and fighters to a four-engined bomber. This diversity of effort and its amount marks R.J. Mitchell for the genius he was.

His assessment is supported by the more dispassionate view in Mitchell's obituary in *Flight* magazine:

His versatility will be appreciated when it is pointed out that his productions ranged from heavy, long-range flying boats to tiny single-seat land plane fighters and on more than one occasion he had two or three very different types of aircraft passing through the design stage at the same time, so that he frequently had to switch his mind from one problem to another of a totally different character.

It must be obvious that such an output, in such a short career, implies that a capacity for hard work was one of Mitchell's main character traits. Versatility and lateral thinking had to be allied with a determination to see a concept to its successful conclusion – and on time.

The most evident proof of Mitchell's drive was the series of Schneider Trophy racers from 1927 to 1931 which, although at the forefront of technical knowledge and under severe time restraints, were delivered on time and outperformed rivals in terms of both speed and reliability.

Today, design complexities are such that many might have reservations about the idea of one man completely dominating the design output of a company, but it should be borne in mind that, during the 1920s and 1930s, it was still possible for one man to have a complete grasp of all the detail that went into the making of an aircraft. Alan Clifton, appointed in 1923 as Mitchell's stress man, said, 'R.J. was widely considered the greatest aeroplane designer of his time when one man's brain could carry every detail of a design'. Thus, while the size of his design team gradually expanded, Mitchell, as well as making the main conceptual decisions, was able to oversee and influence all the detailed working out of a project.

Arthur Black has recorded how Mitchell (who was also the company's chief engineer) would appear in the workshop each day and approve or require alterations before moving on to the next project.

Harry Griffiths, who joined Supermarine as a laboratory assistant in 1929, has also left the following anecdote concerning attention to engineering detail, which is also indicative of why Mitchell was so respected in the firm:

In the S-6 the fuel was carried in the mid-portion of the floats and was pumped up through the struts to the engine. In level flight this would have been OK but during the race the aircraft was banked through 80 degrees in order to negotiate the sharp bends of the course and this created such high centrifugal force that the fuel supply would have been cut off. Thus a small header tank was located in front of the engine to hold a reserve of fuel sufficient to maintain a supply during turns, and the pumps were arranged to deliver an excess of fuel. This meant that on the straight part of the course some fuel had to be returned to the float tanks.

A valve on the front of the header tank had two spring-loaded ports which were supposed to split the overflow into … We tried all sorts of combinations of spring-loaded valve flaps, differing pipe sizes and other devices to equalise the flow without success and the race was getting nearer every day.

One Sunday morning, near to exasperation, we were fitting yet another variation when Mitchell came along and stopped to have a look. At the top of the valve housing there was a small hole leading into the tank which was intended to allow air to escape as fuel went in.

He pointed to the hole and asked, 'Why is that there?', and hearing that it was an air bleed was quiet for a few moments. He then said, 'Stuff it up'. I was sent to the stores to get an aluminium rivet of the right size and we hammered it in. We then reassemble the valve in its original form and switched on the pump for a test run.

Eureka – no matter what we did the fuel split into two equal parts!

Also, Alan Clifton has recorded how Mitchell, as chief designer, would also visit the drawing office and study the drawing in some detail, his head on his hands, thinking rather than speaking. Questions would produce discussion among a small group which would gradually gather round until some conclusion was reached. Mitchell would then move on to another board to repeat the process.

Griffiths has also has left the following observation:

When a problem was being discussed in the drawing office he would stand by the drawing board listening to all the arguments as to what should be done – on these occasions he had the habit of rolling a pencil back and forth on his hand (it was always a very black pencil!) – and when he had heard enough he would push everyone aside, draw a few lines on top of the existing drawing saying, 'This is what you will do,' throw the pencil down and march back to his office.

Ernest Mansbridge, who joined Clifton in 1924 to work on stressing, remembered Mitchell for a similar method of dealing with a problem – by calling in the leaders of various areas and getting them arguing among themselves. He would listen carefully, making sure that everyone had said what he wanted to, and then either make a decision or go home and sleep on it. Joe Smith, who became chief designer after Mitchell, put the matter in this way: 'His work was never far from his mind, and I can remember many occasions when he arrived at the office with the complete solution of a particularly knotty problem which had baffled us all the night before'. In fact, Mansbridge expressed the suspicion that with many problems, Mitchell's discussions were basically to check that he had not overlooked anything and that, otherwise, he had already reached a decision.

A member of the Schneider Trophy team, Flying Officer R.L.R. Atcherley, has also given a similar assessment of Mitchell from a pilot's point of view: 'He was always keen to listen to pilots' opinions and never pressed his own views against theirs ... He set his sights deliberately high, for he had little use for "second bests". Yet he was the most unpompous man I ever met.'

It ought, however, to be mentioned that his very pragmatic willingness to listen to all points of view was not matched by a readiness to bear fools gladly. Most accounts mention his shortness with those who did not get his message quickly enough. For example, Joe Smith said:

R.J. was an essentially friendly person, and normally even-tempered, and although he occasionally let rip with us when he was dissatisfied with our work, the storms were of short duration and forgotten by him almost immediately – provided you put the job right.

Mitchell's condition after his operation for bowel cancer in 1933 exacerbated his testiness, but unfortunately for those working with him, he had kept his ailment private. Even before then, it was not unknown for him to contemptuously flick aside a drawing that did not satisfy him and even to tear it into shreds if it particularly displeased him; and his secretary, Miss Vera Cross, reported that he had no time for those who did not measure up to his standards. Nor did he encourage interruptions when deep in thought at his drawing board, as Joe Smith has recalled:

A mental picture which always springs to my mind when remembering him, is R.J. leaning over a drawing, chin in hand, thinking hard. A great deal of his working life was spent in this attitude, and the results of this thinking made his reputation. His genius undoubtedly lay in his ability not only to appreciate clearly the ideal solution to a given problem, but also the difficulties and, by careful consideration, to arrive at an efficient compromise.

One result of his habit of deep concentration was that he naturally objected to having his train of thought interrupted. His staff soon learned that life became easier if they avoided such interruption ... If you went into his office and found that you could only see R.J.'s back bending over a drawing, you took a hasty look at the back of his neck. If this was normal, you waited for him to speak, but if it rapidly became red, you beat a hasty retreat!

On the other hand, Beverley Shenstone, Mitchell's chief aerodynamicist, reported that he found Mitchell 'very gregarious – when out of the office', and, indeed, in his younger days, he was part of a high-spirited management group not unknown for 'serenading' a rather pompous business manager in the early hours of the morning. There are various later accounts of practical jokes, including Mitchell's dismantling of a colleague's bed when staying at a hotel and his setting fire to another's notes while the latter was giving a speech.

It is also recorded that when his brother visited Southampton, he took him out for a drink at a pub frequented by Supermarine workers, who were not at all disconcerted by the arrival of their boss. His lack of 'side' and, outside work hours, his readiness to be 'one of the boys' was complemented by his taking an active part in the firm's sporting activities – particularly tennis and cricket. Nevertheless, only the breezy RAF Schneider Trophy pilots called him 'Mitch'; in the works, 'R.J.' was the limit of familiarity.

On the domestic front, Mitchell's son, Gordon, remembers that his father was 'damned difficult to live with' and that there were sometimes 'some pretty awful rows'. On the other hand, Denis le P. Webb, who had joined Supermarine in 1926, also recalled the less stormy side of Mitchell's character. When still a very junior apprentice he found that Mitchell 'was friendly and pleasant' and that he put him completely at ease. It was quite obvious that R.J.'s successes had not gone to his head, and they never did. 'Later, if he saw me foot-slogging over to Southampton and he was making his stately way in his Rolls-Royce, he would not be above offering me a lift.'

Flying Officer Atcherley spoke in similar terms: 'He was a man with an alert and inquisitive mind, and in spite of his very considerable attainments in the world of aircraft design he was always ready to crack a joke or take on anyone on his own wavelength.'

In the presence of strangers or women (he left interviews of female staff to others), a certain remoteness was the result of shyness, and he had a slight stammer which increased his dislike of public speaking – something that was demanded of him more as his reputation as a designer increased. Nevertheless, Smith remembered that he could also be charming, with 'an engaging smile which was often in evidence and which transformed his habitual expression of concentration'.

Mitchell's son has also left a boyhood anecdote which relates to this 'concentration'. Having been shown round his father's workplace, he was asked how he had got on and, to his reply that he had enjoyed it, his father responded, 'I don't care a damn whether you enjoyed it, I want to know what you learned.'

Harry Griffiths has supplied a reminiscence of Mitchell which encapsulates some of his apparently contradictory character traits and foibles:

R.J. was human like the rest of us – he could be moody, but in general he had a pleasant personality and I always had the impression that he was somewhat retiring yet he was decisive and when necessary could be very firm.

He had a small personal staff consisting of a clerk, two typists and an office boy – they were all loyal to him and understood his moods. When any unwanted visitor asked to see him he would tell his staff, 'I'll see him in ten minutes' and they knew that this meant, 'Get rid of him!' It worked well until a new typist arrived and the visitor was ushered in after precisely ten minutes! It only happened once.

I've already said that his office was immediately over the laboratory and occasionally he would come downstairs to see Arthur [Black] and would always stop and ask how I was getting on. Sometimes these visits would be to ask the boss if he fancied a game of golf and off they would go for the afternoon. On another occasion he came and played merry hell because the office was untidy, although in fact it was no worse than usual.

Sir Robert McLean, the managing director of Vickers (Aviation), summed up Mitchell's complex character, 'He was a curious mixture of dreams and common sense'. His wife had to become accustomed to his talking at one moment and the next being miles away, and she soon learned to contact his secretary when preoccupation with some design problem led to the evening meal at home going cold. Practical matters such as money were left to her and she would hand out cash for his personal use and replace it as required. And as Vera Cross grew into her job as his secretary, she soon organised his very imperfect filing system, learned how to prevent interruptions, and also relieved him of the main burden of correspondence, which he hated – although she had often to wait beyond office hours before letters were signed.

Apart from seeking a mental break from the inevitable minutiae of aircraft design, or the later demands of becoming a director of the firm, by taking time off for golf, he would, on a nice afternoon, also slip away for a few hours' sailing. This absenting himself is not necessarily at variance with previous accounts of his fierce work ethic but must surely have been a necessary part of the otherworldliness that Sir Robert spoke of. Bearing in mind his well-known concentrated stance at his drawing board, as described by Smith earlier, and the intuitions that pre-figured his many ground-breaking designs, Yeats' lines about prominent persons in history put the matter rather well:

> His eyes fixed upon nothing,
> A hand under his head.
> Like a long-legged fly upon the stream.
> His mind moves upon silence.

THE BEGINNINGS

Given Mitchell's capacity for hard work and, in a more authoritarian time, given his willingness to listen to the views of the team of experts he collected around him, a description of his early years will, nevertheless, show how unexpected – one might say, inexplicable – was his emergence as the man behind the aircraft which contributed so significantly to winning the Battle of Britain.

Reginald Joseph Mitchell was born on 20 May 1895 at 115 Congleton Road in the Butt Lane district of Kidsgrove. Then, three months after his birth, Reginald's family moved a few miles to Longton, one of the 'six towns' soon to be constituted as Stoke-on-Trent: first to 87 Chaplin Road, in the Normacot district, and then to the nearby Victoria Cottage at 1 Meir Road, Dresden, where he grew up. He died only forty-two years later, on 11 June 1937.

Nevertheless, from 1919, when he became chief designer at Supermarine Aviation, Southampton, his relatively brief career spans the whole development of aviation since the pioneering days until just before the beginning of the jet era.

It is worth recording that on 17 December 1903, the year when Mitchell began elementary school, the Wright brothers made the first powered aircraft flights, lasting less than one minute in duration. Only six years later, aviation progress was such that Blériot made a stir by flying across the Channel, and aerial activity came to Britain quite soon afterwards, with Alliott Verdon Roe being credited with making the first flight by a British designed, built and powered aircraft on 12 July 1909.

In the same year, air shows were organised in Doncaster and Blackpool and, in 1910, the young Mitchell must have been caught up in the local interest in flying as crowds flocked to aviation meetings which took place closer to home at Wolverhampton and Burton-upon-Trent. Even nearer, a Wright machine was put on display at the Hanley Park fete in the same year.

By this time, Mitchell was just turning 15 and his enthusiasm for the air would have been further stimulated by the flight of Louis Paulhan in a Farman biplane, which passed no more than 12 miles west of the family home on the way to winning the *Daily Mail* London–Manchester competition. Two years later, another early aviator, Gustav Hamel, came to nearby Stafford and to Stone, for which special trains were organised, and he also came as near as Longton for the Whitsuntide fete.

The young Mitchell was known to have had a passion for building model aircraft, no doubt informed by press photographs and the displays of the very earliest aircraft, particularly the successful machines by the Wright brothers, Farman and Blériot. But an account that Mitchell's models 'swooped and dipped' (which full-size machines seldom do outside airshows), would seem at variance with the approach of a lad who, at the age of 16, made his own lathe and, later, a dynamo. It would seem more likely that his obsession would be directed more technically towards understanding the principles of aerodynamics, as exemplified in straight, level flight – a good preparation for his first Supermarine aircraft which had to satisfy the Air Ministry inspectors that it could 'fly itself' for at least three minutes.

There was a short-lived aircraft firm nearby at Wolverhampton (the Star Aeroplane Co., which in 1910 offered a monoplane based on the Antoinette aircraft and a biplane based on the Farman type), but there is no evidence that the young Mitchell ever visited it. And, even if this had been countenanced by the family, any such precocious visiting of manufacturers with longer-term prospects, such as Sopwith or Shorts, would have involved travelling considerable distances from Stoke-on-Trent. At this time, even motor transport was in its early stages: the year of Mitchell's birth saw the very first car journey in Britain and Herbert Austin began car building in Britain ten years later, when Mitchell was about to go to Hanley High School.

But at least the young boy had the advantage of a good educational background, as his father, Herbert Mitchell, a Yorkshireman, had moved to the Potteries to become a headmaster at Longton. Mitchell also had the advantage of a more practical influence, as his father subsequently became a master printer and, eventually, a managing director of a printing company.

In view of the aesthetic aspects of his design work, discussed later, it should perhaps be mentioned that Reginald's younger brother, Billy, was to set up his own business, designing patterns for the local pottery industry, and that his nephew, Jim, became an artist whose aviation prints of his uncle's Spitfires sold widely.

It is also noteworthy that, having decided to read all the novels of Walter Scott while still a schoolboy, Mitchell is reported to have persevered to the bitter end, and his father would certainly have approved of Reginald's sticking to the task, as he was known to demand high standards of conduct and application.

Similar perseverance was required when Reginald took his first major step away from his father's world and towards his own future career, being apprenticed in 1911 to the locomotive engineering firm Kerr, Stuart & Company, in Fenton, another of the Potteries towns. Shipbuilding, bridge building or textiles might just as well have provided a suitable preparation for the world of engineering at that time, and the local locomotive maker would have seemed to offer just as good and as stable a career beginning. By the time Mitchell finished his apprenticeship to the company, their narrow and standard gauge engines had been sold as far afield as California, Chile, Mexico, China and India (examples are maintained at the Talyllyn, West Lancashire and Leighton Buzzard Railways).

Whatever his future career prospects, Reginald's early training in the work-shops must have been a culture shock to a lad brought up in a middle-class environment (including the works of Walter Scott). Returning each day covered with the oil and grime of the engine sheds was not to his liking and he was all for abandoning the apprenticeship, but his father would have none of it and Reginald stayed on. At least he won one minor victory when his foreman likened the tea that Mitchell had made to urine (or words to that effect). The gentleman was much better pleased with a second mug which Reginald had personally doctored accordingly.

Looking back from Mitchell's later appointment as assistant works manager at Supermarine with its no-nonsense working practices (see later), one can see that these early days were not wasted. More important, however, was his move to the Kerr, Stuart & Co. drawing offices and his attending the Wedgwood Burslem Technical School for evening classes in engineering drawing, mathematics and mechanics. This more cerebral work clearly matched his potential better, as he was awarded one of three special prizes presented by the Midland Counties Union.

By the time he was 21, he had completed his apprenticeship and the First World War had been raging for two years. He made attempts to join the forces but his engineering training was considered more useful in civilian life. Initially, he undertook some part-time teaching at the Fenton Technical School, but his interest in flight (which had also been expressed by the keeping of homing pigeons) then took the form of the fateful decision to apply for the post of personal assistant to the managing director of the Pemberton-Billing aviation works at Woolston, Southampton.

This small company was fully engaged in the war effort, particularly with land planes, although their main interest lay in marine aircraft, and so Mitchell was not only applying for employment in a relatively esoteric form of engineering but also in the doubly remote one of seagoing aircraft. One might say that this type of product was triply remote, as 'hydro-aeroplanes', as they were then called, were less developed than the early land planes. It was only in March 1910 (when Reginald was nearly 15) that Henri Fabre made the first take-off from water by a powered aircraft and in the January of the next year that Glenn Curtiss took off from water in San Diego with a more practical hydro-aeroplane.

The first British aquatic events took place in 1911 at Cavendish Dock, Barrow-in-Furness, where there were several none-too-successful attempts with a converted Avro land plane. Shortly afterwards, on 25 November, another converted Avro machine made the first, more successful, take-off and alighting on water in Britain, with the newly formed Lakes Flying Company of Windermere, which was to be contracted by the Royal Naval Air Service for the development of seaplanes (much to the annoyance of author Beatrix Potter and Canon Rawnsley, founder of the National Trust).

As Blériot had already flown across the Channel two years earlier, it was clear that efficient machines dedicated to water operation were yet to be produced, despite the obvious advantages of large, readily available (and flat) stretches of water. Accordingly, Jacques Schneider sought to encourage their development by offering a trophy for hydro-aeroplanes. The first competition for the new trophy, on 16 April 1913, produced only four contestants, three Frenchmen and an American, and their aircraft all betrayed their land plane origins.

At the time of the second contest on 20 April 1914, Mitchell was exactly one month from his 19th birthday and still an apprentice to the locomotive engineering firm in Fenton, but, if his mind had already been turning to aviation as a career, the primitive state of watergoing aircraft and reports of the first two Schneider Trophy contests could hardly have been encouraging to his family – of those aircraft which managed to cross the start line, only four out of nine had completed the course.

The First World War then brought such civilian competitions to an end, but at least it saw a significant increase in the development of aircraft and of water-cooled British aero engines. Aeroplanes were now becoming sufficiently reliable to play a significant part in warfare – mainly in fighter, reconnaissance, target and gunnery spotting duties – so the demand for aircraft for the war effort now made a career in aviation at least something of a prospect for the young Reginald Mitchell. Nevertheless, it was an unexpected and bold decision at that time for a provincial lad to take a train to the (then) remote south coast for an interview at the Pemberton-Billing flying boat firm at Woolston, engaged in making machines even more unfamiliar than the new-fangled motor omnibus.

His work colleagues later noticed his apparently intuitive feel for which aerodynamic shape would work, and so his early design of model aircraft must have somehow generated an instinct to head for the unknown world of aviation in the same way that an exceptional person fifty years later, with all the insouciance of youth, would have struck out for a place in the space industry. No doubt his keenness to involve himself in this new industry and his youthfulness overcame any misgivings he might have had when he saw what a small-time and underfunded operation the company was at that time. On being offered the personal assistant position, he instantly asked for his belongings to be sent down to him.

The following extract from G.A. Cozens' manuscript 'Concerning the Aircraft Industry in South Hampshire' describes the humble beginnings (1913) of the firm at Oakbank Wharf, Woolston, which Reginald Mitchell joined three years later:

Supermarine [as it was soon to be known] seems to have begun almost by accident and in the early stages the unpredictable nature of the firm's founder [Pemberton-Billing] and his equally colourful general manager [Scott-Paine] might have diverted the destiny of Supermarine in any one of several directions. The factory was in a part of Mr Kemp's boatyard just above the Floating Bridge on the Woolston side of the River Itchen, and a number of strange contrivances were built there. Mr Kemp often said that it was he who kept the little firm going, and indeed the works facilities like the sawmill were very useful and the workforce, who were largely the Kemp boatyard men at the start, were versatile and able to carry out some unusual projects.

(G.A. Cozens lived close to these works in the early days of the company, and was a school friend of one of their workers as well as a neighbour of Henri Biard, their long-serving test pilot. He has left some fascinating, often anecdotal, information concerning the local aircraft industry, particularly on the subject of Supermarine. The author believes that this extract, and the others following, while sometimes inaccurate, deserve to be more widely known.)

THE NIGHTHAWK AND OTHER EARLY AIRCRAFT

Many accounts state that Mitchell joined Supermarine in 1917, but we find, in *Sea Flyers*, C.G. Grey writing that Mitchell 'had been discovered by Mr Pemberton-Billing as a competent draughtsman and later Hubert Scott-Paine put him in charge of the design department'. Noel Pemberton-Billing was no longer the owner of the company when it became Supermarine in 1917, and the *Flight* and *Aeroplane* obituaries to Mitchell in 1937 both stated that he joined the company in 1916. Also, a surviving works drawing of the PB 31E Nighthawk, relating to the central nacelle, its gun mountings, and the various cable runs, is initialled 'R.J.M.' and dated 18 September 1916.

The young Mitchell, builder of small model aeroplanes, must have felt that any misgivings about moving, alone and so far from his family and home, were forgotten, at least temporarily, when he arrived at Pemberton-Billing Ltd and saw this aircraft – a 60ft-span monster quadruplane, standing nearly 18ft high. It was completed and first flew (presumably with the control cables and gun mountings drawn by Mitchell) in February 1917, some months after Pemberton-Billing Ltd was bought by Hubert Scott-Paine, on 20 September 1916. It was he who adopted the old firm's telegraphic address for the new firm – Supermarine Aviation Works Ltd.

The first version of the Nighthawk machine was the PB 29E of 1916 which had been devised in response to the frighteningly new bombing raids by German airships. In order to reach and patrol at the heights attainable by these invaders, an aircraft with a large wing area was required. The usual biplane principle for lightness of construction was applied with a vengeance and resulted in its quadruplane configuration. It crashed not long after its delivery to naval pilots for handling trials but, soon afterwards, the young Mitchell was working on a new version of this 'gunship'.

Just as Mitchell's career ended with, and was brought to the attention of the wider public by, the creation of a land-based fighting machine, the Spitfire, so his design career, devoted mainly to marine aircraft, started with a non-maritime fighting system. The 962sq. ft wing area of the PB 31 was designed to support the weight of a Lewis gun in the nose and, unusually, a non-recoil 1.5-pounder cannon mounted in the top wing pylon, together with another Lewis gun. Equally unusually, there was also a 5hp engine and generator installed in the fuselage to power a movable searchlight at the very front of the aircraft for the purpose of searching out airships at night.

Under a well-known American test pilot of the day, Clifford B. Prodger, the new aircraft was found to reach 75mph and to have a landing speed of only 35mph, but it also took one hour to reach 10,000ft, as its two 100hp Anzani engines proved not to be powerful enough. Mitchell, therefore, must have learned swiftly how aircraft designs were, more than anything else, at the mercy of engine technology.

Meanwhile, the problem of successfully combating the German Zeppelins had been solved by 1917 with the development of an explosive bullet that enabled sufficient oxygen into the airship's hydrogen bags for them to be ignited by an incendiary bullet. As both these bullets could be loaded into the gun magazines of conventional aircraft, the development of the heavily armed Nighthawk was not required.

An earlier Pemberton-Billing design, the PB 25, had fared better with an order for twenty machines, and these had a configuration that was to become very familiar to the later Southampton firm: the small biplane with a pusher engine. Like the PB 29 and PB 31 it was also a land plane, as the First World War mainly encouraged the development of aircraft to operate over the battlefields of France and Belgium.

The embryo company gained further valuable design and structural information as their wartime effort involved repairing and building of other firms' aircraft – in particular, twelve Short S38 and twenty-five Norman Thompson NT 2B seaplanes.

PB 31 Nighthawk under construction (R.J. Mitchell fourth from right?). (Courtesy of Solent Sky Museum)

Design experience of a more direct sort soon came Mitchell's way for, when he joined the company, it was completing an order to build some Short Type 184 floatplanes. The association with this firm was particularly important as those firms granted licences to manufacture Short's products were supplied with full sets of blueprints and had to send their staff to the parent company for instruction. Other budding aviation firms such as Fairey, Westland, English Electric and Parnall also benefited from this arrangement – not to mention the untrained Mitchell himself.

The company had also just finished two flying boats specified by another pioneer aviation group, the Admiralty design team. This unit, from the Royal Naval Air Station at Eastchurch, together with the one at the Royal Aircraft Factory at Farnborough, represented much of the contemporary ability to tackle aerodynamic and structural problems in a scientific manner.

This first group of people was responsible for designing for the war effort and as a result, they were instigators of the Handley Page heavy bomber and a range of Sopwith aircraft that were originally intended for naval use. Most of the early theoretical work, in particular the seminal *Handbook of Stress Calculations*, came from this source, and so it was again fortunate for the young Mitchell that some of this leading team was sent down to the works at Woolston to draft out the details of new naval machines.

The first two aircraft completed to Admiralty designs were accordingly known as 'AD Boats' and again exemplified the pusher biplane configuration of the PB 25. With the addition of the PB type of wing superstructure to the new boat-like hull, there begins to appear the general flying boat formula that was to inform Mitchell's Commercial Amphibian, Sea Eagle and Sheldrake, and which led up to his well-known Walrus. Significantly, the particular details of flying boat hull construction also came to the new company: F. Cowlin, the technical supervisor at the Royal Naval Air Station has recorded how he went down to the Pemberton-Billing firm and 'learned a great deal about hull design from Linton Hope, who joined the section for a time while we were engaged on the AD Boats'. The lines and structure laid down by this well-known yacht designer became the basis of all the wooden flying boat structures that Mitchell subsequently utilised and were, in fact, a considerable advance on that of the current naval flying boat, the Curtiss-derived Felixstowe.

Cozens also supplies relevant information on very early hull construction and workforce conditions:

> In 1914 the firm built the small flying boat PB I which was a credit to the workforce, and indeed it was judged to be the best example of aircraft construction at the 1914 Olympia Aero Show. This applied to the workmanship but unfortunately not to its performance.
>
> The PB I hull was of round construction, built by small boat methods with closely spaced wooden ribs of half inch square section like girl's hoops, joined by longitudinal stringers and covered by two layers of mahogany or cedar wood planking, laid so that the outside layer was sloping the opposite way to the inner layer, this was known as 'opposed diagonal planking'. There was a layer of doped fabric between the layers and the whole fastened by brass screws or copper nails and in some cases the nails were turned over and clinched or riveted over a small washer …
>
> The machine never flew and it is likely that the aerodynamics were wrong. The engine and propeller were at 15 degrees to the centre line of the hull, so that it seemed the machine was intended to lift off as soon as the engine opened up. In any case, the engine was not powerful enough to maintain flight.
>
> An *Echo* 'Letterbox' contributor wrote to say that his father, who was working at Supermarine, was told to fetch an axe and Pemberton-Billing, after looking at the beautiful machine for a long while, broke it up.
>
> When the Great War started, the Supermarine factory [not yet so named] became involved in repairing damaged floatplanes from Calshot and no doubt the workforce gained experience from this, but the PB 9 was a typical Supermarine venture. It was almost certainly a copy of the successful Sopwith Tabloid which had won the first [second] Schneider Trophy at Monaco the

year before but there is no doubt that the plans for the PB 9 were little better than something on the back of an envelope, probably hastily drawn and given to a foreman, who was then told to do his best. However, the simplicity of the design and the construction did not detract from its performance and it handled well.

Scott-Paine trusted his men to work well and he knew that they were the ultimate ones in whom he had to put his faith, it was long before the aircraft inspection board was established. The remarkable thing about the PB 9 was that it only took seven days from the time the project was set in motion until it was finished, and a number of stories have been put forward as to how this was done, but the way Scott-Paine worked was always the same, and instead of locking the men in until they had finished, as one story said, he agreed with the foreman on a price for the job and left it to him. No doubt the men did work hard and long, but in their own way. They took into account the fact that there was inadequate lighting in the factory, and worked as much as possible during daylight, and they also had in mind the fact that the copal varnish had to dry and other practical things, so that, whatever the urgency was, the practical considerations were what counted …

The worst fear of craftsmen employed at Supermarine was that by some mischance his job could be lost for the most trivial accident, even breaking a thin twist drill meant a walk to the storekeeper to ask for a new one and the payment of a fine. The problem was that the flying boat hulls were

Supermarine workers with tools of their trade. Mitchell is standing (and looking uncomfortable?) third from right. (Courtesy of P. Jarrett)

fastened by rows of small screws which meant drilling through two layers of cedar ply and into the rock elm ribs, which was hard on drills, but before long the men solved the trouble by making their own drills. They cut knitting needles or piano wire into lengths of about 2in and annealed one end, hammered the tip flat and hardened it like a spear. Each man had an Archimedes drill with a simple brass chuck which could be purchased as a part of a fretwork set and was suitable for drilling small holes at awkward angles because it was light and only needed a straight [manual] push and pull action …

By 1917, the first of twenty-four production AD machines to be ordered was undergoing acceptance trials for the navy, and so Mitchell, who obviously knew much more about heavy locomotives than lightweight wooden aircraft, had ample opportunity to see the flying boat construction techniques employed as the rest of the aircraft were built. As Harald Penrose of Westland wrote:

> The Admiralty had found floatplanes too dependent on smooth water; they were interested in the far heavier flying boat hull which in the Linton Hope approach consisted of a double skin of mahogany planking with fabric in between, with rock elm strips forming almost circular ribs, longitudinally stiffened by closely spaced stringers.

However, the hydrodynamic aspects of aircraft hull design were in their infancy. The early test pilot, John Lankester Parker, described his first acquaintance with the AD Boat as follows:

> Not only did it develop a formidable porpoise at a very low speed, but nothing I could do would prevent it turning in ever smaller circles to the right, despite the fact that my passenger went out on the port wing-tip to keep one float well and truly in the water.

Aside from structural matters, the young landlubber Mitchell would have now discovered that it was one thing to design an efficient yacht hull but quite another to produce one that would easily plane over the water and break free from its suction in a controllable manner. On the one hand, a calm sea and no wind might prevent the currently low-powered aircraft from being able to 'unstick'; on the other, it might 'porpoise' in a series of bounces over waves until the right flying speed and angle might be achieved. (The standard First World War Felixstowe flying boat embodied an alternative type of hull with a flying boat fore body married to a conventional land plane fuselage of longerons and struts, but it was found to need additional planking, which affected its performance as well as its flying trim. It was no better a performer on water than the AD Boat.)

The unlikely transformation of a lad from the middle of England trained in locomotive engineering into a designer of sea-based aircraft became possible because Scott-Paine must have recognised something about the applicant for the post of personal assistant when he stood before him – although his particular engineering background was not necessarily a drawback. For example, H. Fowler had been apprenticed to the Lancashire and Yorkshire Railway, and had become the chief engineer of the Midland Railway before becoming the superintendent of the Royal Aircraft Factory, and S.T.A. 'Star' Richards had been apprenticed to the Great Western Railway before becoming Handley Page's personal assistant and, later, his chief designer in 1922. In those days, Mitchell's mathematical and drafting skills would have been his predominant qualification, and applicants for Mitchell's post would most probably have only offered aviation experience as an additional bonus.

Whatever had singled out the young man from the Midlands for his first post, first impressions were clearly not ill-founded, for Mitchell was promoted to assistant works manager in 1918, and his improved financial position now enabled him to travel back to Stoke and to marry Florence Dayson (headmistress of Dresden Infants' School) at St Peters church, Caverswall, on 22 July. It is a striking fact that Florence was eleven years older than himself, which suggests that the young Mitchell's mentality was attracted to that of a mature professional woman and that he was displaying at an early age a single-mindedness and determination that overrode what, particularly at that time, must have seemed to his parents an unusual match.

One must also imagine that some of Mitchell's early domestic evenings were spent in study, as the same year saw the issue of *HB 806* by the Technical Department of the Air Board which contained a full account of the mathematical methods employed by the department. And while a contemporary designer admitted that in such vital matters of weight/strength ratios and, therefore, safety margins, 'we did it by guess and by God', more theoretical information became available for Mitchell to study in 1919, with the publication of *Aeroplane Structures* by A.J. Pippard and J.L. Pritchard, and *Applied Aerodynamics* by L. Bairstow.

The recent appointment of a professor of aerodynamics at Cambridge also marked the development of something approaching a systematic and scientific approach to the new technology. But how far the Southampton company was to become a significant part of it was by no means certain. The Society of British Aircraft Constructors did not have a committee member from Supermarine and the strong British presence at the 1919 Paris Air Show did not include any machines from Mitchell's firm.

However, at least the new assistant works manager was busy early in 1919 with another seaplane project, namely the conversion of some of the surplus Admiralty AD Boats into civilian passenger-carrying aircraft. Ten of these two-seaters, which were in storage, were purchased back from the Admiralty with a view to offering trips from Southampton to various seaside resorts on the Isle of Wight, and drawings were prepared for the installation of four passenger seats and a more economical engine.

The name 'Channel' indicates the very modest transport ambitions of the company and, in fact, the first of the passenger services was only between Southampton and Bournemouth. But at least Supermarine had the distinction of obtaining the first British Certificate of Air Worthiness for a passenger-carrying flying boat in the August of 1919. The flights, which cost 4 guineas single and 7 guineas return, were claimed to be the 'First Flying Boat Passenger Service in the World'. (One of the pilots employed was Captain Henri Biard, who was to test all of Mitchell's designs in the next ten years.)

Several trips were also made to Cowes, but only for passengers who had missed the regular ferry. However, by the August of 1919, regular services to the Channel Islands as well as to the Isle of Wight were begun, weather per-mitting, in addition to joy rides at various venues on the south coast when opportunities arose. During that year, the steam-packets ceased operation in sympathy with striking British railway men and the Channels finally lived up to their name by operating a service to Le Havre for the duration of the dispute, so providing a precedent for the government's use of the RAF to pro-vide a newspaper service between London and the provinces during the 1926 General Strike. The service, costing £25 return, began on 28 September and came to an end on 5 October; the Bournemouth Service gradually petered out with the onset of winter.

Cozens' account of the AD Boat conversion and of the early, spartan Supermarine passenger services deserves recording:

The conversion from wartime use to peacetime was fairly basic and consisted of taking out the engine and fitting a more economical Beardmore 160hp which caused the machines already prone to porpoising, to be even worse. The rest of the preparation was to paint out the RAF roundels, but not the red, white, and blue colours on the twin rudders, and SUPERMARINE was painted on each side of the bow.

When the pilot and his mechanic got to Bournemouth, or Brighton, or Bognor or elsewhere they planned to operate they anchored and relied on the local boatmen to ferry out the passengers and help with the refuelling. This enterprise started in July and continued through August and September ...

Towards the end of September they were modified to carry three passengers and began flying to Le Havre and so became the world's first international flying boat service.

The experience gained in September and October 1919 by flying passengers across 114 miles to Le Havre led Supermarine to plan further efforts for 1920 and they built more machines with a higher bow to give the passengers more protection against wind and sea. They were known as Channel IIs but the passengers still had an uncomfortable ride on many occasions and I remember seeing a Channel come up to a buoy just below the Floating Bridge [at Woolston] and although the three people were wearing flying coats and helmets they looked wet and miserable as they got into a boat that was rowed out to meet them ...

Captain Biard was yet another of the colour[ful] personalities that Supermarine seemed to attract and he was an extremely good pilot, indeed he flew every kind of aircraft as it was produced, be it single or twin engine, light or heavy, on land or sea. One of the little known but important things he did was to train pilots for flying boats, something that even experienced land pilots found difficult, and it was a common sight to see a Channel taxying up and down Southampton Water trying to take off, or landing with a series of bounces.

Four of the AD Boats had gone to an embryo Norwegian Air Service and Mitchell was obviously also involved with the company's further purchase of another six AD Boats. Some were converted to a three-seat trainer version

A Channel II 'on the step'. (Courtesy of Solent Sky Museum)

and some were bought by the Norwegian Government for use with their Naval Air Services. There then followed a Mark II conversion with a more powerful engine, and three such aircraft went to the West Indies in 1920; two more were modified for photographic reconnaissance and used for surveys of the Orinoco Delta in Venezuela. Other Channels were also delivered to the New Zealand Flying School, the Royal Swedish Navy, Chilean Naval Air Service and the Imperial Japanese Navy (the visiting Japanese officials were reported to have been particularly impressed by the handling of the Channel in strong winds and heavy seas by Henry Biard, who in 1919 had now joined the company as test pilot).

Meanwhile, a separate Air Ministry had been created, the RAF Staff College had been established at Cranfield and a marine training section and aerial navigation school had been set up at Calshot, only a few miles from the Supermarine factory. Thus, although Supermarine's order book was soon not always to be so healthy, the newly married Mitchell, with the optimism of youth, could see signs of an expanding new transport system and of government support, particularly for its military aspect, and he could look forward to his company taking a full part in these developments.

Looking out over the River Itchen, down to Southampton Water and then, in his mind's eye, to the destinations of the recent Supermarine aircraft – Europe, Japan, South America, or New Zealand – the industrial smog of Stoke-on-Trent must have seemed a long way away, particularly as in 1919 he had just been appointed chief designer, at the age of 24. Other quite young designers must have had similar dreams: Chadwick, at A.V. Roe, was 26 and Pierson, at Vickers, was 27. Sopwith, Fairey, Handley Page, Folland and Blackburn were all in their early 30s, leaving Oswald Short at 36 and De Havilland at 37, as the old men of the group.

The total dominance of land plane travel nowadays ought not to disguise the fact that, to Pemberton-Billing, to Scott-Paine or to Mitchell, the marine side of aviation would have been seen as the most natural of developments, not the minority, specialist aspect of the business that it is today. With motor travel in its infancy and with Britain being surrounded by sea, flying boats represented the most obvious next step in the development of long-distance travel. Trade depended on boats and they were essential to serving the far-flung outposts of the British Empire. Britain also had numerous reasonably sheltered stretches of water offering generous expanses for machines which, as we have seen, might be erratic in behaviour and need a considerable area for take-off.

Although the original Pemberton-Billing firm had diversified into land planes as part of the war effort, the original intention of the enterprise was best signified by its telegraphic address 'Supermarine'. The owner's original

Reginald Mitchell at the time of his marriage, 1918. (Courtesy of Solent Sky Museum)

goal had been to produce 'boats which fly and not aeroplanes which float', and when the new company was formed the new managing director chose for the company name 'Supermarine' (literally, the opposite of the more familiar 'submarine') to indicate where his hopes for future aircraft also lay.

But despite the foresightedness of Jacques Schneider in 1912, and despite the fact that the First World War had given a more than considerable boost to aircraft and engine design, the marine side of British aviation had not profited so well – with the large Felixstowe reconnaissance flying boat being something of an exception. Unfortunately, the Felixstowe had not been a Supermarine product, and dwindling new orders, especially for marine aircraft, were beginning to suggest a less prosperous future for the company that Mitchell had joined.

As we shall see, the third Schneider Trophy competition offered the chance of good publicity for marine products, including Supermarine's, but the entries showed what little progress had been made in this area of aero design at the time that Mitchell became chief designer.

2

EARLY DAYS AT SUPERMARINE

MITCHELL'S EARLY MODIFICATIONS

The early Pemberton-Billing/Supermarine interests had ranged from the very large Nighthawk land plane to a small naval 'scout' for the navy, and Mitchell's early design experience was closely involved with this latter fast seaplane type and its various transformations.

The company's interest in the naval interceptor type had begun with an Air Ministry requirement, N1B, for a fast manoeuvrable single-seat seaplane or flying boat fighter, with a speed of about 100mph at 10,000ft and a ceiling of at least 20,000ft. It was required particularly to combat the German Brandenburg fighter seaplanes which had been operating over the North Sea.

The resultant 'Baby' had been designed by F.J. Hargreaves, who was in charge of the drawing and technical offices at Pemberton-Billing when Mitchell joined the company and who continued for a little while after the company became 'Supermarine'.

Hargreaves' close liaison with the Admiralty Air Department produced an aircraft with what appeared to be a dangerously small fin and rudder, typical of aircraft drawn up by this design team (presumably in response to accidents caused by over-ruddering which could lead to spinning in) but the Baby was, in other respects, a more 'in-house' response to the ambitious N1B specification.

This machine did not go into production because the First World War ended, but, as Mitchell had joined the firm in 1916 and had then been involved at least

ABOVE: The N1B Baby. (Courtesy of E.B. Morgan)

PREVIOUS: The Supermarine Sea Lion II. (From a painting by the author)

with the Nighthawk, it is entirely likely that he had had some design input in the three N1B airframes that were going through the works. By the time of the Armistice, N59 (see photograph opposite) had been completed and was being evaluated by the navy and N60 was largely complete. The third, N61, was under construction, and was most probably (in view of its extensive departures from the N59 Baby design) the one modified for entry in the 1919 Schneider Trophy competition – in the hope to gain some very useful publicity from an event to be staged by Great Britain, the winner of the previous event in 1914. The modifications were such that it was renamed the Sea Lion I.

Sea Lion I

The particular configuration of this aircraft suggests that the modifications to the original Baby design were largely those of Hargreaves. The fin and rudder were enlarged in a shaping not followed later by Mitchell. Likewise, the base of the latter was used as a water rudder, the inter-plane struts were splayed outwards and the balanced ailerons on the top wing had an inverse taper. Also, the hull was decked to keep down spray, and so the front of the fuselage was far less sleek than Mitchell's later Sea Lion II and Sea King II.

In appearance, the design suggested that the man with overall responsibility for the aircraft seemed to have favoured rugged seaworthiness rather than speed through the air. As such, when it came to selecting the three aircraft to represent Britain in the Schneider Trophy competition, the Sea Lion was the Royal Aero Club's third choice over the slightly faster Avro 539A, possibly in order to hedge its bets because of the already proven seagoing qualities of Supermarine machines.

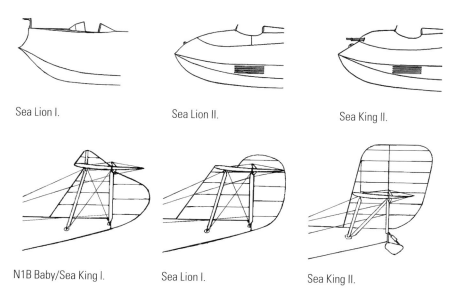

Sea Lion I.   Sea Lion II.   Sea King II.

N1B Baby/Sea King I.   Sea Lion I.   Sea King II.

The Sea Lion I at Bournemouth for the 1919 Schneider Trophy Competition. (Courtesy of Solent Sky Museum)

But, by the time of the Schneider contest, Hargreaves had left the company and it was Mitchell who would have assumed last-minute responsibility for this aircraft. He accompanied Scott-Paine, the new managing director of Supermarine, in one of the company's current Channel flying boats to the event at Bournemouth.

Unfortunately, the 1919 Schneider Trophy contest was an embarrassing non-event because of incompetent organisation and fog, and so was of no help to Supermarine, whose publicity for the Sea Lion I had clearly indicated Supermarine's hopes of military orders:

> This machine, which is said to be the fastest flying boat in the world, is a small, fast, single-seater, designed primarily for war purposes. With the Napier 450hp engine, 2 hours' supply of fuel, and a load of 140lb of guns and ammunition, the speed is 147 miles per hour. The hull is guaranteed to stand up to practically any weather, and the machine itself may be looped, rolled, spun, or put through any of the manoeuvres demanded by aerial fighting.

The next two Schneider Trophy events took place in Italy, but flyers from other countries apparently did not feel inclined to finance entries to what was not yet a major aeronautical event. Meanwhile, Supermarine persisted with their fighter flying boat concept with the Sea Kings.

Sea King I

Little is known about Mitchell's involvement in the Baby N60 version, bought back from the Air Ministry, but it seems likely that it became the Sea King I.

This aircraft appeared at the 1920 Olympia Aero Show, and therefore after Mitchell's appointment as chief designer, but how long it had been in existence in this guise before this date is unknown. Certainly, a photograph from the show reveals a direct repetition of the earlier, apparently inadequate, tail configuration and so represents past practice rather than the future.

Perhaps its original specification, with a Beardmore 160hp engine, was not expected to present directional problems, given that the Baby flew with a 200hp Hispano-Suiza engine, but the proposed fitting of a 240hp Siddeley Puma engine might have produced some design responses from Mitchell, such as the fin and rudder of his later Mark II version (see drawings on p.35).

One speculates that, at this time, the profitable modifications to the AD Boats (also bought back from the Air Ministry) had so preoccupied Supermarine that a N60 Baby, unmodified by Mitchell, was sent to the Olympia Aero Show essentially as a marker for the company's continuing interest in the naval fighter scout concept.

C.G. Grey has left an interesting memory of this display:

> As one stepped onto the stand one had a feeling of confidence that here were people who really knew what they were at in the sea-flying game. Hubert [Scott-Paine] and his two brothers wore yachting caps and double-breasted reefer jackets and looked real sailor men. Their helpers wore jerseys … and in each corner of the stand was a large coil of tarred rope flemished-down in workmanlike seafaring fashion.

Despite the showmanship, there is little information about the aircraft having been flown, although the following publicity for this aircraft would seem to imply that control, even with the original less powerful engine, had not been found to be quite adequate. It also reveals that the company was hoping to sell to the many private flyers that the First World War had produced if military orders could not be achieved:

> The 'Sea King' is a small fast single-seater which for general purposes follows the structural methods of the 'Channel Type' boat. With its 160hp Beardmore engine it puts up a speed of 96 knots, so that it is either a thoroughly sporting little vehicle for the single or unhappily married man, or is a useful small fast patrol machine for naval work along troublesome coasts. Its chief difference in design from the 'Channel Type' lies in the fact that it only has a monoplane tail of the depressing kind [inverted camber] and so takes rather more flying on the part of the pilot than does the bigger machine.

Had there been any sales, perhaps Mitchell would have wished to modify the tail surfaces but, unfortunately neither the military nor the 'single or unhappily married man' came along to buy one, so it had to await the Mark II development by Mitchell two years later.

Sea King II

In response to the continued Air Ministry interest in a fighter design for ship-board use, Mitchell now produced an amphibian version of the Baby/Sea King I machine, designed, as company publicity proclaimed, as:

> A high performance fighting scout, specially adapted for getting off gun-turret platforms of capital ships, or getting off and landing on the decks of aircraft carriers. The strength and design of the hull are such that it can oper-ate on and from the water under any weather conditions in which it would be possible to operate any other sea craft [boats] of equal size.

It was produced in 1921 and so its modifications can be attributed entirely to Mitchell and, indeed, it bore distinct evidence of his taking over the design department at Supermarine.

The most obvious revision of the earlier design was the more generous fin and rudder area (see sketches on p.35), as the 160hp Beardmore engine of the Sea King I was now replaced by the much more powerful 300hp Hispano-Suiza engine; and it would appear from the Supermarine publicity quoted on the following page that Mitchell's redesign had a noticeably beneficial effect.

The Sea King II. (Courtesy of E.B. Morgan)

As with his Seal, which also flew in 1921, the tailplane was now placed almost midway up the fin. The retracting gear of the Seal was again utilised, and a Seal type combined tailskid and sea rudder was also employed. The aerodynamically balanced ailerons and rudder of Hargreaves' Sea King I were again abandoned, and at the same time Mitchell devised a very simple method for the removal of the undercarriage system which enabled the company to offer the choice of flying boat or amphibian with minimum extra production costs.

In other ways, the Sea King II followed the example of previous Supermarine designs, particularly the Linton Hope hull construction, 'with built-on steps, which can be replaced in case of damage ... divided into watertight compartments, the top side being of single-skin planking, covered with fabric, treated with a tropical doping scheme'. The wing-tip floats were the same full depth type as employed on the Baby, Sea Lion I and Sea King I, and the tailplane outline was similar to that of the Sea Lion I or the Seal II but with the lower position of the latter. Its reversed camber continued the Baby method of counteracting nose-down tendencies at higher engine revs.

The Supermarine description of this version of the single-seat flying boat fighter type also draws attention to its flying qualities as well as to the many practical features now incorporated by the designer (a theme that would become familiar in the Mitchell story):

> The manoeuvrability of the 'Sea King' Mark II is one of its most important features. It can be looped, rolled, spun, and stunted in every possible way. Longitudinally, the machine is neutral, and flying at any speed throughout its entire range either with engine on, gliding, or climbing, no load is felt on the control stick. This balance has been obtained entirely on the stabilising surfaces, and no mechanical adjustment by the pilot is required ...
>
> The engine, a 300hp Hispano-Suiza, is mounted in a streamlined nacelle, which contains oil tank, radiator and shutters, piping, controls, etc. The whole unit is very accessible and the engine can be replaced very easily.
>
> Interchangeability and ease of upkeep and repair have been carefully studied. The complete wing structure, including power unit, can be removed from the hull by withdrawing eight bolts. The wing structure consists of top and bottom centre sections, and top and bottom planes of equal span. One set of struts are carried on either side of the centre-section. The top planes have a dihedral angle of 1° and the bottom planes one of 3°. The engine unit is carried on two sets of inwardly inclined N struts, and can be removed and replaced without interfering with any wing structure member ...

The amphibian undercarriage, which can be removed by the undoing of ten bolts in all, folds up under the wings, and when folded is well clear of the water. It is raised and lowered by a worm and bevel gear.

The pilot's cockpit is in the nose of the boat and gives an almost unobstructed view in every direction. The equipment consists of a complete set of instruments, anchor and cable, bilge pump, towing fairleads and make-fast cleats, boathook, engine and cockpit covers, towing bridle and lifting slings, 'Pyrene' fire-extinguisher, Lewis gun and six double trays of ammunition.

The Sea King II was designed and built in six months and made its first flight at the end of 1921. *Flight* repeated the Supermarine claims that it had a degree of manoeuvrability equal to that of any contemporary conventional fighter and that it was inherently stable, allowing hands-off flight in reasonable weather conditions.

One interesting feature of the design was a vertical tube through the fuselage which conducted air from the slipstream down to just behind the rear planing surface, in order to prevent a vacuum forming behind the step when accelerating for take-off. This form of ducting had been employed earlier by water speed enthusiasts. However, as there are no other reports of Supermarine again using this approach to the problem of efficient 'unsticking' from water, it must be assumed that no advantages were found to this device.

Once more, no orders were received, but there was some further development in 1922 and 1923 in respect of Sea Lions II and III.

MITCHELL'S SEA LIONS

In 1922, the Air Ministry issued a specification for a single-seat fighter capable of operation from aircraft carriers or as a floatplane, but the Sea King II, being a flying boat, was not in the reckoning in spite of a potentially competitive performance. The winner of the Air Ministry contract was the Fairey Flycatcher with, eventually, a profitable 196 machines being built. It had a slightly higher top speed over the Sea King (133mph compared with 125mph) and it was just as aerobatic. Additionally, its short span allowed it to be struck down to aircraft carrier hangers without folding wing arrangements, and its extensive aileron-cum-flap arrangements produced very low minimum take-off and landing speeds.

With hindsight, it might be seen that the days of a flying boat fighter were numbered, but the managing director of Supermarine was still determined to continue with the type and decided again to seek publicity for it by entering another version of the aircraft in the 1922 Schneider Trophy contest. Another, more patriotic, reason might have been to prevent the Italians from winning the trophy outright, which, according to the rules of the contest, they could do in the forthcoming competition: it may be recalled that, after the inconclusive Bournemouth event of 1919, the Italians had had fly-overs in the following two years.

Meanwhile, with France winning the Gordon Bennett Cup for land planes for the third consecutive time, permanent possession of this trophy had gone to the winning country and thus, importantly for Mitchell, brought to an end the main international prestige race for land planes. Thus, despite the poor attendances and even worse performances in the Italian fourth and fifth events, the Schneider Trophy contest had ended up as the main international speed competition remaining. This would obviously suit Supermarine very well because of their concentration on seaplanes and, in particular, on flying boats. The recent contests had set the trend for entering this type of machine rather than the improvised land plane.

In addition, the rules had been changed in 1920 to encourage a more practical type of aircraft, rather than an out-and-out racer. 300kg of ballast had to be carried, and this had favoured flying boat designs. Although the ballast requirement was dropped the next year, it was replaced by a watertightness test in which the aircraft had to remain afloat, fully loaded, for six hours. Again, this rule tended to suggest the continuing suitability of the flying boat for the trophy contests, and it must have been noted that the recent Italian designs of this type which had failed in the previous two competitions had actually only done so because of over-ambitious power upratings.

Sea Lion II

Despite the omens favouring flying boats, any such Supermarine entry was unlikely to have any financial backing from its government, unlike the firms from Italy. The uncertain financial outlook of the Supermarine Company at this time was such that when its managing director entered an aircraft, he had obtained the loan of a Lion engine from the manufacturers, a high-speed propeller, petrol and oil from other companies, and had negotiated a reduction in insurance rates.

Scott-Paine also negotiated with the Royal Aero Club for the payment of the competition entry fee and, shortly afterwards, a payment of £100 towards the company's costs. Nor was the company intending to incur the cost of designing and building an entirely new airframe. The fuselage of the salvaged Sea Lion I was with the Science Museum at South Kensington and so the fuselage of their Sea King II (which, in any case, was aerodynamically cleaner) was utilised.

Mitchell, no doubt having taken note of the sleek Savoia S.13 at Bournemouth, aimed for increased speed by making the entry of the fuselage, which was originally shaped to house a gun (see drawing on p.35), somewhat smoother, and his simplified method for the removal of the undercarriage system also enabled the hull to be easily stripped of the extra weight and drag of this item. Also, as the Napier replacement developed 150hp more than the Hispano-Suiza engine that had originally been fitted, he was able to decrease the area, and therefore the drag, of the wings by reducing their width.

Another modification, probably mentioned to Cozens by his neighbour, Biard, was necessitated by the pilot's refusing to test fly the aircraft until the rear fuselage had been stiffened up (see extract below). Again, in response to the extra power of the engine, an additional increase in fin area was called for. Mitchell achieved this with the least expenditure of time and money by merely modifying the vertical surfaces above the tailplane. The leading edge of the fin was given a pronounced forward curvature which proved to be effective but certainly won no prizes for elegance.

Although Supermarine's finished entry was very much based on Mitchell's Sea King, it was named the 'Sea Lion', thus drawing attention to the name of the loaned engine. It was also designated a Mark II, to distinguish it from Hargreaves' earlier design but, as a result, it has misleadingly suggested that it was a direct development from it, contrary to its actual pedigree described earlier.

There have been many accounts of the 1922 Supermarine win, and so the following relatively unknown contemporary Cozens' extract is given:

The price for such an engine was beyond the means of such a small firm as Supermarine but on the other hand they offered an ideal opportunity to test its capabilities, so Montague Napier loaned it, knowing that if the Sea Lion won the publicity would repay him. It was a water-cooled twelve cylinder with three banks of four cylinders in arrow formation, short and sturdy for its power output. Each cylinder barrel was a separate casting but the cylinder heads were in a single casting for each block so that the whole block bolted together into a well-designed and efficient unit, sturdy and reliable. Each cylinder had its own copper water jacket. The tall Mr Pickett was responsible for the engine fitting and his skill and experience served Supermarine well for many years.

When the new racer was taken out on to the quay and the powerful Napier was run up Captain Biard took one look at the vibrating tail and said he would never fly that aeroplane, but, with typical press-on spirit the riggers wrapped doped fabric round the fuselage and made the whole unit stiffer. The next crisis was when the Italians advanced the date of the race by fourteen days and bad weather cut down Captain Biard's chances of getting used to the Sea Lion, and this was further jeopardised by a forced landing which began with the engine cutting out over the Dock. However, when he had had a few more flights he was satisfied and the speed and handling proved very good, indeed it was faster than any flying boat or seaplane of that time.

The Sea Lion II. (Courtesy of E.B. Morgan)

Then, with the limited time available, it was doubtful if they could get the Sea Lion to Naples in time but the General Steam Navigation Co. agreed to take it and it was hurriedly dismantled, put into a crate and on to a lighter, and one of Ray's tugs took it down to the Solent and the freighter *Philomel* lifted it on board and took it to Naples.

Pre-race spying and counter-spying on both sides was all part of the event. This atmosphere continued throughout the whole series and it was the policy of each competitor to arrive at the start of a competition with a machine that was ahead of its rivals by virtue of some secret and outstanding advantage which was not revealed until it was too late for anyone to copy. In the case of the Sea Lion this meant that the wingspan was cut down to an absolute minimum and as the trials at Woolston had been curtailed even Captain Biard was not too well practised as to the machine's behaviour.

He kept his speed down in the practice flights but was quietly getting used to the course and conditions, and his engine fitter, Mr Pickett, tuned up the engine to the higher temperature of the Bay of Naples, so that when the race started Biard was reasonably prepared ...

When Captain Biard and his victorious team came to the Floating Bridge with the great prize held above their heads no one bothered whether it was a cup or a trophy – everyone called it a cup, certainly Scott-Paine. I had parked my bicycle outside the Woolston Picture House and I saw the Supermarine workers run down to meet them. They had taken the two swivel chairs from the office and fixed them to poles and they lifted Captain Biard and Scott-Paine in the chairs shoulder high and carried them round the works.

One suspects that Mitchell's relatively recent arrival in the firm at the time, as well as his temperamental self-effacement, account for there being no mention of him in the celebrations.

Mitchell's machine not only won the Schneider Trophy race for Britain at an average speed of 145.7mph, but it also gained the first Fédération Aéronautique Internationale (FAI) world records for seaplanes:

(i)   Duration – 1hr 34min 51.6sec
(ii)   Distance flown – 230 miles
(iii) Fastest time for 100km closed circuit – 28min 41.4sec (130mph)
(iv)   Fastest time for 200km closed circuit – 57min 37.4sec (129.4mph)

Although city dignitaries had turned out in full ceremonial dress in recognition of Supermarine's international success, subsequent lack of military interest in the Sea Lion type must have been a disappointment to the company. Also, its designer would have been only too aware that the Savoia S51 which was beaten in this last competition would, in all probability, have been the winner had it not been for the handicap of a damaged propeller. In fact, it was powered by an engine only two-thirds as powerful as the Napier Lion and, on 22 December of that year, it captured the world speed record for seaplanes at a speed of 174.08mph.

The Sea Lion III

As the next Schneider Trophy contest was to be held in England, it was to be expected that Supermarine would be only too happy to capitalise on their 1922 publicity by competing, successfully it was hoped, without the cost of overseas travel and accommodation. Indeed, the new venue decided on was to be Cowes, less than 20 miles from the Supermarine works at Woolston.

While the order for a second batch of five Seagulls in February 1923 was to be welcomed (see Chapter 3), it was still only a part of the government's minimal financial lifeline to the ailing aircraft industry, and only with the large-scale production of the Southampton, which began two years later, might Supermarine have felt justified in the cost of designing and building a one-off specialist racer. As the top speed of the Sea Lion II was significantly less than the record-breaking S51, the company did not immediately respond to the challenge.

When Scott-Paine was persuaded to submit an entry, he confined himself to asking his chief designer to do his best with the Sea Lion II airframe. Mitchell designed new wing-tip floats, which offered less frontal area, mounted them on streamlined struts and added fairings around the main strut attachment points. Because an extra 75hp was available from the new Lion engine, the rudder and fin were increased in area, with the resultant redesign looking somewhat like

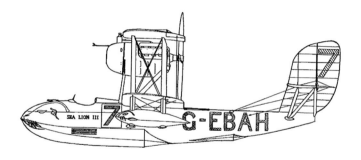

The Sea Lion III.

an extension of his early Sea King II outline, and certainly less improvised than that of the Sea Lion II.

Mitchell fitted the uprated Napier Lion III engine and radiator into a more streamlined nacelle, and the more powerful engine also allowed for a reduction in the wingspan by 4ft; he also had fairings made behind the two hull steps – which might have inhibited the ability of the aircraft to take off, had it not been for the extra power now available.

Mitchell's changes could hardly prevent the Supermarine machine from showing its, by now venerable, pedigree – as did the other two eventual British contenders. The Blackburn Pellet was, like the Sea Lion, based on a hull built for the 1918 N1B contract, and the third British entry, from Hawker, was to be a further uprated version of the Sopwith Schneider machine of 1919.

One feels that the rather whimsical sea lion motif painted on the nose and floats of the Supermarine entry (see photograph on p.46) was almost a self-deprecating gesture in the face of the expected serious opposition from overseas: in 1921, the US Navy had contracted with the Curtiss Aeroplane & Motor Co. for the development of a pursuit (fighter) plane, the CR-1, which was soon to be tested in the newly established Pulitzer Trophy Race for land planes; it won, at an average speed of 176.6mph. The US Army then took over the development of the Curtiss racers which, in 1922, were fitted with one of the great aero engines in aviation history, the Curtiss D-12, whose frontal area was about 50 per cent less than that of the rival Napier Lion. The winning of the 1922 Pulitzer race was also due to the incorporation of radiators flush-mounted on the wings, and to the use of metal propellers (the usual, thicker, wooden blades were beginning to prove inadequate for the newer engines which were producing tip speeds approaching the speed of sound).

As it turned out, no Italian competitors were sent to the competition and, on the day of the race itself, one of the French machines which had survived the flight to England, collided with a yacht and the damage to its hull put it out of the contest. Another was unable to compete because of engine trouble. Also, the Blackburn Pellet had sunk after serious porpoising on take-off. Then the surviving French CAMS withdrew on the second lap of the flying section, because of engine trouble and damage to its right elevator on take-off. So, perhaps the obsolescent Supermarine aircraft might have some success, after all. It all depended upon the quality and seaworthiness of the less robust American floatplanes.

Of the three machines that finished the competition, the Curtiss CR-3 floatplanes came first, with an average speed of 177.3mph, and second, with an average of 173.46mph. Despite 75hp more, Supermarine's flying boat could only manage an average of 157.17mph and a poor third placing. Clearly, the usual European formula of an engine mounted above a flying boat hull was no longer likely to be the best configuration. The American approach, despite the drag of floats, allowed for an engine to be neatly cowled so as to merge into the streamlines of the fuselage. There was also a formidable engine and propeller combination and flush-fitted wing radiators to take account of. The Curtiss CR-3 design also limited the number of other drag-inducing items to sixteen struts, with twenty wires, despite the extra penalty of float attachments and bracings, whereas the Sea King/Sea Lion I designs Mitchell had inherited required thirty-three struts and forty-two wires.

The Supermarine Sea Lion III at Cowes, 1923, with test pilot Biard in the cockpit.
(Courtesy of Solent Sky Museum)

At the end of the race, Biard made a consolatory gesture by pulling up to a considerable height and then descending in a series of tight spirals before alighting in front of the disappointed British crowd. Afterwards, Scott-Paine praised the Napier engine 'that would have gone on for ever' but said that he needed 'to apologise to Captain Biard because we did not give him a good enough machine'.

The Sea Lion was returned as N170 to the Marine Aircraft Experimental Establishment at Felixstowe with its undercarriage and sea rudder/skid now replaced, but its career was short-lived, owing to its extremely lively take-off performance. As Biard had said, 'It was an interesting sensation; you switched on the engine, and before you could count 1,2,3,4 fast – she was flying.'

Unfortunately when a service pilot, Flying Officer E. Paul-Smith, took the Sea Lion over, he apparently did not take sufficient notice of the warning that the machine tended to lift off before flying speed had been reached. As a result, he took off, dropped back onto the water, rose to about 40ft, stalled again and dived in. Paul-Smith was killed – a sad precursor to Lieutenant G.L. Brinton's death in the S6A eight years later (see Chapter 5). The Sea Lion was too extensively damaged to be considered worth repairing.

This incident, on 25 June 1924, marked the end of Supermarine's attempts to interest the Air Ministry in the seaplane scout concept but, importantly, it also led to Mitchell's later searches for a design specifically dedicated to the Schneider Trophy competition.

MITCHELL'S FIRST FULL DESIGN

Although he had contributed to the Nighthawk of 1916, assisted chief designer Hargreaves until he left in 1919 and was involved with various conversions of Admiralty-inspired aircraft, R.J. Mitchell was first responsible for an overall design with the 'Commercial Amphibian' of 1920. It is surely worth considering this design in some detail, not only because it represents the beginning of an illustrious career, but also because it showed immediate promise.

The first aircraft involved in commercial flying after the end of the First World War were conversions of military machines – like the Channels, which we saw earlier were by no means well suited to their new roles. And so it was in March 1920 that the newly formed Department of Civil Aviation at the Air Ministry announced two competitions for commercial designs 'of British Empire origin' to promote 'safety, comfort and security' in air travel. With a view to developing international travel (bearing in mind the few airfields available, compared with large stretches of water worldwide) one of these competitions was specifically for amphibian seaplanes, with a first prize of £10,000 and a second one of £4,000.

It was not surprising that Supermarine asked Mitchell to design an entry for the seaplane competition, which was to commence on 1 September of that year. By later standards, the requirements for a successful entry were extremely modest. In the amphibian category, these included seating accommodation for a minimum of two passengers, a range of 350 nautical miles at 1,000ft and at a speed of not less than 70kt, and a load carrying capability of 500lb, to include passengers and life belts but not including crew. There was also a requirement for a flight of three minutes to check if the machine would fly itself unaided. Additionally, the entries were required to clear balloons at a height of 25ft from a 400-yard take-off run.

From the experimental station at Felixstowe, the amphibian competitors were required to take off, pass as high as possible between marker boats 600 yards from the start buoy and land at the experimental (land) station at Martlesham Heath. Taxiing on water had to include figures of eight, taking off and landing in rough weather, and mooring out for at least twenty-four hours in moderate weather. These marine trials were not unlike those that Mitchell's Schneider Trophy racers had to complete before the actual flying contests, and of course reflected the same concern to develop aircraft that had practical seagoing features.

The Commercial Amphibian

As the Commercial Amphibian was the first comprehensive design by Mitchell, it is surely very understandable that the end product would be a conservative one. Even if Mitchell had been an experienced aircraft engineer at this time, he would still, in all probability, have followed previous best practice, in view of the little theoretical data that was available and as wind tunnel experimentation or tank testing (for flying boat hulls) was not available to his small firm.

Also, there were only about twenty weeks separating the announcement of the competition and the trials, leaving little time for innovative thinking. *Flight* reported that 'for the Martlesham amphibian trials the Supermarine Company designed and completed a flying boat in all respects in ten weeks from the time when the first drawing was commenced to the time the aircraft was in

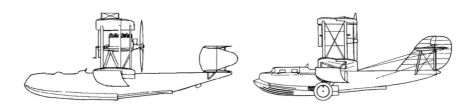

Channel.   Commercial Amphibian.

the air, the actual building time being four weeks'. Not surprisingly, therefore, Supermarine described the new design as 'practically a "Channel" type boat, with a wheeled undercarriage hinged on each side' although, in fact, side views show considerable changes in the Mitchell design (see opposite).

Based on a Channel airframe, the Commercial Amphibian had a biplane layout in which similar dimensions of height and length were adopted, and the sea rudder was similarly placed – vertically below the leading edge of the tailplane – but now converted to act also as a skid when taxiing over land. The wing-tip floats were also of the Channel sort and the oval hull and the general arrangement of its built-on planing surfaces employed the Linton Hope/Channel principles of hull construction.

On the other hand, Mitchell also incorporated features of a much smaller aircraft, the Sea Lion I. The fin and rudder outlines were similar, although a proportional increase in surface area above the tailplane allowed the designer to provide a more symmetrical appearance to the fin. And the Sea Lion's outwardly raked inter-plane struts were repeated in the new, and larger, machine. (Thereafter, it would seem that Mitchell preferred the simplicity of equal span wings supported at right angles by the inter-plane struts.)

Between the Amphibian's struts there were canvas stabilising screens, full length between the inner pairs and quarter length between the middle ones. These screens were relatively uncommon by this time, but survived on several later Supermarine designs as well as on the Channel and Sea Lion, perhaps mainly to protect the engine and propeller from spray on take-off or landing; but it was the present machine that was most extensively fitted with them and, in this respect, it did not look particularly like an advanced design.

As many of the features from the Channel and the Sea Lion I were, thereafter, abandoned by Mitchell, the present design can be regarded as something of a 'time capsule', a summing up of earlier practices rather than a statement of the way forward. But Mitchell also showed an early instance of boldness by abandoning the biplane tailplane and twin rudders of the Channels (still evident in the Handley Page HP 42 of the 1930s) in favour of a single fin and tailplane.

It is also worth noting that the competition rival, Vickers Viking III, went through three more variants before the Mark VII, the Vanellus, appeared five years later with a more modern-looking single tailplane. Also, Mitchell's rudder was a departure from the minimalist approach of previous Admiralty-inspired rudders – perhaps his work alongside Hargreaves on the Sea Lion I had had some influence in this respect. Additionally, Mitchell significantly remodelled the nose with a prominent boat-like entry to counter spray, a feature which was to prove successful in his future Sea Eagle, Scarab and Seagull designs.

The Commercial Amphibian with ground handlers, at Martlesham. (Courtesy of E.B. Morgan)

A further novel feature was Mitchell's design for a retracting undercarriage, necessitated by the Air Ministry competition being for amphibian aircraft only. At this time an American land plane, the Dayton–Wright RB-1 Racer, had an innovative fully retracting landing gear, designed especially for the Gordon Bennett race of 1920, whereas the present concern was merely to lift the wheels out of the water, in order to facilitate take-off and alighting.

The first European design of this sort was the Sopwith Bat Boat of 1913, which, like the present rival, Viking, had a mechanism that rotated the wheels upwards and forward. Supermarine's concern for 'boats which fly' offered no previous experience of retractable undercarriages for Mitchell to call upon, and so it is noteworthy that for his specially designed mechanism he chose a geometry that displaced the wheels outwards rather than forward – thus avoiding any change of trim when the wheels were moved up or down. (Mitchell retained this sideways mode of retraction for all of his future amphibian undercarriages.)

One other particular feature of the Commercial Amphibian must also be mentioned: the enclosed passenger cabin. The competition's intention of ascertaining 'the best type of Float Seaplanes or Boat Seaplanes which will be safe, comfortable and economical' might have seemed to make an enclosure for passengers inevitable, but it should be noted that the other two amphibian entries had open cockpits for their three passengers, one seated next to the pilot and the other two side-by-side behind. Open cockpits at this time were the norm, and they saved weight, but they were far from ideal in northern climates – one remembers Cozens' previous description of Channel passengers looking 'wet and miserable as they got into a boat that was rowed out to meet them'.

Supermarine's concern that passengers should not be in the open might also have resulted from the experience of Supermarine's pilot, Henri Biard, on 30 September 1919, on the Channel Flying Boat Service to Le Havre. He recorded that the weather that day had deteriorated into a gale with sleet and snow but, with a flask of rum supplied by Scott-Paine for heating, a Belgian financier braved the open front cockpit of the aircraft. The cold was such that the passenger, a Captain Alfred Loewenstein, tried to pass the flask to the rear cockpit but only succeeded in causing the spirit to blow back into the pilot's eyes. Thereafter, the passenger tried to raise an umbrella, obviously unaware that the aircraft slipstream might blow it into the propeller – which was directly behind the two men. As it was impossible to converse with the passenger in the front cockpit, Biard had to resort to hitting Loewenstein about the head, whereupon he disappeared into the well of the cockpit. (The Belgian was to become a 'mystery of flying', on 4 July 1928, when he disappeared from a Fokker FVII over the Channel.)

This glimpse into the pioneering days of aviation might seem amusing (though not to the pilot at the time), as was the arrival of the Supermarine crew for the Air Ministry competition dressed in heavy jerseys and sea boots. The Vickers people turned up in sailor hats with 'Viking III' in gold on their hat-bands and the *Aeroplane* at the time noted that 'all the competitors treat the affair as a very good joke'.

Despite the apparently light-hearted or amateur approach to the event, the same correspondent did also note that the amphibian entrants hedged their bets by reserving their maritime tests until last 'as they wanted to complete land tests before chancing damage to their machines by awkwardly handled launches or a sudden squall'.

No significant adjustments or replacements to the Mitchell aircraft were required, despite its one-off design and the short notice of the competition. Supermarine publicity made the most of it, saying that the aircraft 'put up an extraordinarily good show in that competition. It completed all the tests satisfactorily, and was only beaten by competitors with engines of considerably greater power in the matter of speed and climb'. The judges also noticed with approval an effective tiller arrangement for steering while taxiing on water, the other equipment for sea use, and the way in which the shape of the forward part of the hull kept spray off the passengers' compartment.

It might be expected that the company's marine experience would produce such comments. Equally, it might not be too surprising that Mitchell's novel undercarriage gave rise to criticism for being none too clean, from the mechanical and maintenance points of view. The lateral control of the Commercial Amphibian was also considered not immediately responsive enough and the wing-tip floats too small and inadequately secured. On the other hand, a comparison between the slab-sided Consuta plywood sheet approach of the Vickers entry and the boat-like hull that Mitchell inherited, showed that he had had the good fortune to have joined a firm with a technique of hull building that was to stand the firm and its chief designer in good stead for the rest of that decade.

An increase of nearly 150sq.ft of wing area compared with the Channel had been estimated by Mitchell as being needed to address the performance specifications of the competition and to lift the additional weight of the amphibian landing gear. A more powerful but heavier engine, the Rolls-Royce Eagle VIII, was also used. Unfortunately, the result was a loss of certain competition points when, otherwise, it would have taken first prize.

Despite its passenger-carrying capacity of only two – the minimum allowed by the competition rules – the final report on 11 October stated that 'the results achieved for amphibians show that considerable advance has been attained … and the competing firms deserve congratulations on their enterprises' and the second prize money of £4,000 was doubled as 'the proportion of the monetary awards does not adequately represent the relative merits of the first two machines'. (A Fairey floatplane with an added wheel attachment came third and was awarded £2,000.)

One can imagine how the new Mrs Mitchell must have felt at this promising start to her husband's career but, from a technical point of view, it was a modest beginning, to be sure. Nevertheless, as we shall see later, many of its features and its overall performance gave rise to a call from the Air Ministry for a further development of this machine, which led to the Sea Eagles and the Seagulls between 1923 and 1926.

THE SEA EAGLES

The 1920 commercial aircraft competition had been a reflection of the inclusion in the Government's Air Estimates of an allocation for civil aviation (although it represented something less than 2.5 per cent of the total), and in June 1922 the Air Ministry gave approval for an air service between Southampton, Cherbourg and Le Havre. The route, with a subsequent extension to the Channel Islands,

A Sea Eagle with Biard aboard. Note the sea anchor below the cockpit and the original, single fuel tank on the top wing. (Courtesy of E.B. Morgan)

was to be operated by an air service named the British Marine Air Navigation Company, and Hubert Scott-Paine and James Bird of Supermarine were to be its directors. Not surprisingly, the first Supermarine aircraft for this service was already being built when the Air Ministry granted the company a subsidy of £10,000 and agreed to pay £12,000 for aircraft and spares (later revised substantially downwards as the air miles generated were less than the company had expected to fly).

The aircraft designed for this service was named the 'Sea Eagle' as it was to be powered by the Rolls-Royce Eagle IX engine. For this machine Mitchell continued the customary pusher configuration for single-engined flying boats and went back to the more boat-like hull shape of the larger Channel and Commercial Amphibian designs. In fact, the fore section of the Sea Eagle, with its high, pointed prow, enclosed accommodation for passengers, large windows and grab-rails on the roof, resembled a cabin cruiser of the time. As the two planing steps were also joined by a continuous hard chine which ran three-quarters of the hull length, it embodied, more than any other Mitchell design, the original Pemberton-Billing concept of 'boats which fly'.

Wing folding was again adopted and a forward-folding arrangement was again employed – which reduced the width of the Sea Eagle by 54 per cent, although increasing the length by 15 per cent. This configuration had the structural advantage of siting the folding mechanism at the main spar with no possibility of a wing folding backwards in flight. This arrangement, however, necessitated a cut-out in the leading edge of the wings, which did nothing for aerodynamic efficiency.

Mitchell adopted the practice of gravity feed for the engine of this latest flying boat with apparently few qualms about stability problems, for the fuel tank (and subsequently a second tank) was attached to the top of the wing cen-tre-section. On 28 June, a *Flight* correspondent wrote that that 'this machine represents a great step forward in the development of the seaworthy amphibian' having appreciated a 'most important innovation' that, in place of the usual tank in the hull, 'the main petrol tank has been mounted on top of the top plane, so that direct gravity feed, with its attendant simplicity and freedom from breakdown, can be used'.

The writer also added:

> The fact that the engine is mounted high above and some distance aft of the cabin has resulted in reducing the noise audible in the cabin to a minimum, and as a matter of fact, in the 'Sea Eagle' it is possible for the passengers to converse in ordinary tone of voice, without having to shout to one another. [One remembers Biard's earlier 'communication problem' with Loewenstein in the Channel flying boat.]

One departure from all previous (and future) biplane practice was the use of a pronounced stagger of the two wings, as the weight of the forward passenger cabin and its six passengers necessitated bringing the centre of lift of the top wing well forward of the engine. One notices that Mitchell's usual preference was for the simplicity of directly opposed wings.

The first completed Sea Eagle made its maiden flight in June 1923, and received its Certificate of Airworthiness on 11 July. Two days later, Supermarine entered the new aircraft in the King's Cup Air Race that had been initiated the year before, also to encourage aviation development. As it was a handicapped event, the entry of a commercial flying boat might not seem too strange, but the car-rying of four passengers must have had much to do with the company being mindful of publicity generated by air races. Unfortunately, circumstances involv-ing a burst tyre and its replacement led to the aircraft being disqualified.

On the 5th of the next month, the Director of Civil Aviation at the Air Ministry, Sir Sefton Brancker, came to Southampton and was given a display of the machine's ability to negotiate the (usually) crowded seaway, as well as a demonstration flight. He announced himself to be well satisfied with the Sea Eagle's potential contribution to the development of civil aviation, both in terms of performance and comfort and, along with other senior members of his department, had another flight nine days later.

Particular comment was made on the very sensible placing of the passengers, and in the following publicity the company makes reference to the advantages of this arrangement:

> This machine was specially designed as a commercial amphibian or flying boat for passenger carrying work. It carries six passengers and pilot, with fuel for a distance of 230 miles. Extra tankage is fitted so that the range can be increased by reducing the number of passengers.
>
> The passengers are accommodated in a roomy cabin in the fore part of the hull. This cabin is very comfortably fitted out. Its position in front of the engine makes it very quiet and free from engine exhaust, gases, oil, etc.
>
> It is very efficiently heated and ventilated, and is fitted with sliding triplex windows along the two sides for use in the warm weather. The machine is very strongly built and very seaworthy, and has proved itself quite safe in the roughest of seas usually experienced in the Channel. It is fitted with either a Rolls-Royce 'Eagle IX' engine of 360hp or a Napier 'Lion' of 450hp.

Supermarine's experiences with the Channel service and with the Commercial Amphibian had obviously influenced Mitchell to give considerable thought to the enclosed cabin arrangement, such that one passenger recorded descending into the Sea Eagle and finding 'a delightful little room' that the company had fitted with 'reposeful armchairs'.

Intermittent proving services began in August, and regular daily services between Southampton and Guernsey began on 25 September 1923. As such, it constituted the very first British scheduled flying boat service and was advertised to leave Woolston at 11.15 a.m. and return from St Peter Port at 3.30 p.m. (the French section of the service did not materialise). The service, often with breaks due to bad weather, continued with the Sea Eagles for the next five years, even though the single fare to the Channel Isles was not cheap for the 1920s at over £3 single and £7 return. Compared with boat transport, however, the normal flight time of one and a half hours was very attractive, although in adverse wind conditions it might be almost an hour more.

Cozens has left the following recollections of the Sea Eagle service:

The land planes flying from Croydon to the Continent carried wireless
transmitters and receivers and had the benefit of a simple direction finding
service, by which stations at Pulham in Norfolk and Lympne in Kent and
Croydon could take bearings on an aircraft when its generator was running.
Then Pulham and Lympne passed their bearings to Croydon, who would
plot them, together with its own bearing, and so reach a 'fix' which would be
passed to the aircraft pilot. The Sea Eagles carried the same equipment but
they could not use it for direction finding purposes because they operated
outside the sector where the system could be applied, but they could speak to
their bases at Woolston and Guernsey.

I lived a mile from the Supermarine works and could hear an engine
start, in those days a rare sound and quite distinctive from the riveters at
Thornycroft or the rumble from the coaling wharf in the docks. These were
the main sources of 'noise pollution' at that time. From the front gate I could
watch the machine fly across the Dock Head and then go indoors and pick
up the headphones of my crystal set. Soon I would hear 'leaving the coast at
Beaulieu', and 'passing the Needles', and about 90 minutes later and hoping
the cat's whisker [fine wire detector] had not moved I would hear 'passing the
French coast at Ushant' and sometimes very faintly 'approaching Guernsey
and winding in'.

When the time came for the return trip I would hear the call in the reverse
order, passing Ushant, the Needles, Beaulieu, and 'approaching Hythe and
winding in'. Then I would cycle to the Floating Bridge in time to see the
flying boat taxi up to its mooring. It was the flight engineer who operated the
wireless [which] was powered by a wind-driven generator fixed to the cabin
roof and the expression 'winding in' referred to the trailing aerial, a long wire
with a weight on the end, which had to be wound on to a drum before the
Sea Eagle could touch down …

By this time the airline's operations were carried out from buildings along
the side of the works and the staff were glad to have proper offices instead
of the exposed Jopling's Wharf and along the side of the boat shop the
words 'Woolston to Guernsey in 90 minutes' were painted in blue and white.
The Sea Eagles were finished in copal varnish and white, and the windsock
was an orange colour and the motor boat varnished, making the whole operation smart and attractive …

Nearly four years later, the fleet of three Sea Eagles was down to one. *G-EBFK*
had crashed on 21 May 1924, due to a bird strike, according to Cozens,
and *G-EBGS* was rammed and sunk when moored at St Peter Port on 10 January
1927 (a reward of £10 for the identity of the culprit was never claimed).

A Sea Eagle in Imperial Airways livery at the Woolston terminal. Note the word 'Airport' on the roof of terminal (is this the first use of the word?). It has leading edge cut-outs for forward wing folding, and fuel tanks above the top wing, as well as fixed ladders for passengers and crew. (Courtesy of Solent Sky Museum)

But, for four years, two of Mitchell's machines had not only operated the first scheduled flying boat service in Britain but they also had the distinction of forming part of the basic fleet of the organisation which became part of Imperial Airways and eventually British Airways. On 31 March 1924, Imperial Airways Ltd had been incorporated as the 'chosen instrument' of the British Government for developing national commercial air transport on an economic basis, and the British Marine Air Navigation Co. was one of the four companies taken over for this purpose.

Scott-Paine became a member of the Imperial board of directors and so was able to use his influence to keep the Solent area, and Southampton in particular, to the fore in British commercial flying boat operations. The two Sea Eagles remaining at that time now had their fuselages painted with prominent 'Imperial Airways' lettering.

In the following year, it was reported in the *Aeroplane* that the Sea Eagles, 'during their hibernation have grown another 100hp' and are 'now equipped with Napier "Lions"'. The last of the three Sea Eagles, *G-EBGR*, was finally retired in 1928, thus justifying Supermarine's claims that this type was 'very strongly built and very seaworthy'.

A photograph from a correspondent for the *Aeroplane* showed a Sea Eagle hull at Heston Airport in 1954. At this time, the Imperial Airways marking had been painted out and the extant letters *G-EBGS* were now of a different character from those seen in photographs of the machines when in service. Andrews and Morgan, the authors of *Supermarine Aircraft since 1914*, state that the hull in question was that of G-EBGR, the last survivor of the Eagle fleet, rather than that of the retrieved G-EBGS. Whatever the truth of the matter, *a* hull was presented to the British Overseas Airways Corporation in September 1949 and intended for restoration and display at the new London airport, but nothing came of this proposal and this piece of industrial archaeology was burnt on 13 February 1954.

3

EARLY MILITARY ORDERS

PRECURSORS OF THE WALRUS

The Commercial Amphibian, Mitchell's first success as chief designer, brought an order from the Air Ministry for a military development of the type as part of its policy to assist the struggling aviation companies to stay in business. This was a recognition that British air power needed the support of a healthy aviation industry, especially as the RAF had been in action again with a new military tactic. 'Control without occupation' was a very economical and swift-acting aerial alternative to the employment of army land forces in the policing of colonial and League of Nations mandated territories, and it was used against tribesmen in Mesopotamia, Transjordan, the Sudan and Somaliland, against the Bolsheviks in Russia and against the Afghans on the Indian frontier.

The Air Estimates of that year accordingly allocated £1,389,950 (although far less than the £54,282,064 of 1919) for the purchase of aeroplanes, engines and spares, and recognised that contracts for new, more advanced types would have to be spread around the various aviation firms in order to maintain the technical staff which had been built up. (Sopwith had already turned to making motorcycles, and Fairey, Gloster, Blackburn, Shorts and Bristol were manufacturing bus or car components.)

In order to fulfil the new Air Ministry requirement, Mitchell's next design was to be a three-seat amphibian for use as a fleet spotter, to be extremely seaworthy and to have the lowest possible landing speed with good control in order to land onto aircraft carriers. Mitchell's response was known as the Seal II, presumably with the Commercial Amphibian being regarded as the Mark I predecessor, which had also been a three-seater, as well as being fitted with a retracting undercarriage. However, many design changes show Supermarine's young designer eager to improve upon his previous effort.

Seal II

The Seal II had the outwardly retracting landing wheel geometry first introduced on the Commercial Amphibian, but the detail of the Seal's system shows that something had been learned from the criticisms of the earlier plane's mechanism. The earlier machine had an undercarriage consisting of two steel tubes, hinged below the lower centre-section join with the lower main planes, and the wheels were raised or lowered by sideways movements of a tube in the hull to the wheel axles. The new undercarriage now had a single strut, suspended from the lower wing and braced by two tubes hinged to positions on the hull.

PREVIOUS: Supermarine Scarabs for the Spanish Navy. (From a painting by author)

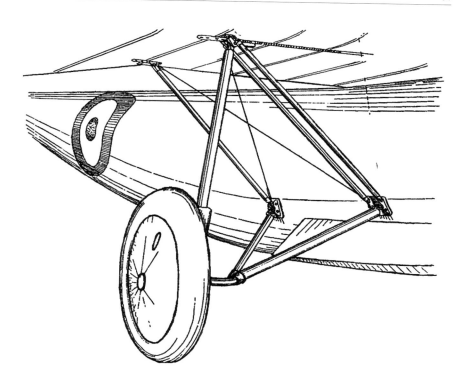

For retraction, the top of this main strut was moved inwards by means of a worm and bevel gear, thus reversing the previous method and siting the retracting mechanism further from the water. It was utilised on all future Supermarine amphibians up to, and including, the Sheldrake of 1927.

Mitchell also improved on the previous aircraft by siting the tailskid/water rudder further back, at the stern-post. This had the effect of increasing the wing incidence during taxiing and so improved the take-off performance (on land at least) which had not been very impressive in the earlier machine. A *Flight* commentator added a further design consideration: 'it is much easier to provide the necessary strength and watertightness than it is with a rudder working in the trunk of the hull. Also the tail loads, which are considerable, are lessened.'

Of the flying surfaces, only the tailplane followed the previous Hargreaves Sea Lion outlines and, although Mitchell now placed the stabiliser lower on the fin, he retained the inverted aerofoil principle. This feature was also continued until 1927, being necessitated by the customary high thrust line of the engine, which caused increasing nose-down forces as power increased. The need for constant back pressures on the stick was thereby reduced or eliminated as cruising speeds were reached.

On the other hand, the wing shape was new and this planform was retained by Mitchell for all his subsequent medium-sized naval aircraft, again, up to and including the Sheldrake (see drawing opposite). But the rearward-folding wing requirement for a shipboard aircraft had not been tackled by the Supermarine Company since the Baby of the First World War, and Mitchell adopted a similar approach – and one which he, again, continued with in military aircraft until the Sheldrake – the forward wing strut at the joint between the wing centre-section and the main plane was doubled so that one of these members carried the weight of the leading section of the wing when folded back.

The need for wing folding also required large cut-outs to be made in the trailing edges of the wings, so that they could fold close to the plane's centre line to keep storage space to a minimum, and the wings were placed further forward than in the Commercial Amphibian so as not to project behind the trailing edges of the tail assembly when folded.

The wing-tip floats, with their decreased side areas, were less clumsy than before and offered less drag, as they could now be carried on struts to the waterline. The pilot was placed well forward and supplied with a machine gun which could be retracted and shielded during take-off and landing. The wireless operator was just aft of the wings and the rear gunner was behind him, with the fuel tanks separating off the pilot from the other two crew members.

A Seal II at the Supermarine slipway, showing retracted undercarriage arrangement.
(Courtesy of Solent Sky Museum)

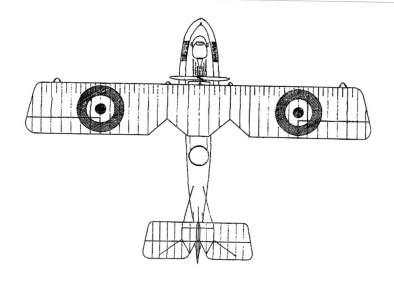

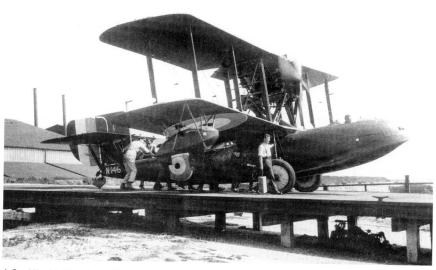

A Seal II with the wing folding cut-outs and new float configuration. (Courtesy of RAF Museum)

Because two of the crew members were placed behind the wings, a trac-tor layout had to be chosen for the engine to prevent the centre of gravity moving too far back. *Flight* believed this to be 'the first British flying boat to be designed as a tractor'. The pusher configuration was also the most obvious way to keep the propeller as far back as possible from the spray at take-off and land-ing. In Supermarine's publicity for the Seal, attention is drawn to this placement, no doubt because of its novelty (at least in single-engined machines):

The engine is the Napier of 450hp. The engine mounting is unusual in that it is of the tractor type. This has been rendered possible by the fact that in this case the greater part of the useful load carried is aft of the wings in the tandem cockpits, and the success of the tractor mounting will allow this type of boat to be arranged either as a tractor in such a case as this or as a pusher in cases where the greatest useful load is concentrated forward. Very great attention has been paid in designing this engine installation to securing accessibility for inspection and adjustment of the engine and its accessories.

One notices the offer of the more conventional pusher layout – presumably in the hope of a civilian version which would not, one might reasonably assume, need a gunner behind the wings. The company publicity also draws attention to the new designer's typical concern with the practicality of his machines – in this case, the ease of access to the engine.

N146, the prototype Seal, first flew in May 1921 and, in the following year, one machine was sold to Japan, who were keen to be kept abreast of Western technological developments. Despite this general lack of orders, the Seal is important in our story as it is the one early Mitchell design that most clearly looks forward to one of his three main aircraft types – the Seagull II to Seagull V/Walrus series of medium-sized amphibians.

Meanwhile, the company had to come to terms with the post-war Anti-Waste League and the resultant Geddes Committee Report, which led to a drastic reduction in government expenditure. The new Secretary of State for Air, Sir Samuel Hoare, reported that in 1923 only 371 front-line aircraft remained, either in the British Isles or abroad, and thus assessed the current situation: 'Orders for military planes had almost come to an end and a demand for civil planes did not yet exist … Only 2,500 men and women were left in the industry and the few firms engaged on machines and engines were on the verge of closing down.'

On the other hand, 'control without occupation' had to be backed up by support for the ailing aircraft industry if there were to be an adequate response from the depleted RAF. Thus it had been decided that, over the next five years, thirty-four new squadrons would be formed, bringing the number up to fifty-two squadrons by 1928. In the event, the total home squadron numbers only rose to thirty-four by the date proposed, but at least the 1923 Air Estimates of £10,783,000 had risen to £16,042,000 by this time.

Seagulls II–IV

The first positive result of the new situation was seen when Commander James Bird, who had taken over Supermarine at the end of 1923, approached the Air Ministry and subsequently received a letter which cautiously suggested that it 'might be inexpedient' to close down the works entirely as Supply & Research were considering an order, 'the exact amount of which cannot yet be stated, but which might approach eighteen machines, spread over the period ending March 31st, 1924'.

A first Air Ministry lifeline came in the form of an initial order for two flying boats of the type Mitchell, in anticipation, had begun developing from the Seal. A more powerful Napier Lion II engine was now envisaged – again in a tractor layout – and the fin consequently increased in area and the wingspan reduced.

Thereafter, two new aircraft with these modifications, N158 and N159, were renamed 'Seagull' and were completed by March 1922. The type was displayed in the same year at the third annual RAF Pageant, Hendon, by which time the wing-tip floats had been redesigned, the wings given a slight sweep back, the ailerons redesigned, and the fin area further enlarged. The number of modifications resulted in these first production Seagulls, in fact, being designated Mark II.

There was one particular modification of the Seal type which ought to be mentioned: the fuel tanks had now been moved from the fuselage to positions under the top wing centre-section, supplying petrol to the engine by gravity feed. In the First World War, the Felixstowe flying boats, which had fuel tanks more conventionally placed in the fuselage, had suffered so many forced landings from blocked pipes and fuel-pump failures that a contemporary report stated, 'our real enemy is our own petrol pipes'. It is a reflection of the very slow pace of aircraft development after the Armistice that Supermarine drew particular attention to their adoption of gravity feed as late as 1923, with the Seagull II.

Previous experience of the high position of the Sea Eagle's fuel tankage would have shown Mitchell that the basic Supermarine amphibian configuration, with a suspended boat-like hull, made possible such new fuel arrangements without stability problems. There was also an additional bonus: as a consequence of moving the fuel tanks from the hull, Supermarine was able to announce that 'inter-communication between crew has been considered fully, and a through passage is arranged for this purpose'. Thus Mitchell was not only solving possible supply problems from petrol in lower positions, but was also making an important step forward in the matter of military crew communication – something that was particularly appreciated when the Southampton flying boat came into service two years later.

In passing, it should be noted that the constructional methods of the Linton Hope hull that Supermarine had adopted conferred another advantage, in that there were no internal bracings or structural bulkheads to be weakened when opening up a passageway between the pilot and the other members of the crew.

A competitive test on HMS *Argus* between the Seagull and the Mark VII version of the Viking (whose predecessor had competed successfully with Mitchell's Commercial Amphibian in 1920) had found in favour of Mitchell's machine and, thereafter, Vickers concentrated upon land planes.

An RAF order for five Seagulls, N9562–N9566, was received in February 1923 and the Undersecretary of State for Air, the Air Vice-Marshall and the Director of Research visited the Supermarine works on 23 February 1923, to view the progress of the order. The Ministry were sufficiently pleased with the aircraft that a further order for five additional Seagulls (N9603–N9607) was received, and this was followed by a requirement for another thirteen (N9642–N9654). These aircraft equipped No. 440 (RAF) Fleet Reconnaissance Flight, and six were placed aboard the aircraft carrier HMS *Eagle*. An additional machine was again sold to Japan.

Further orders for the Seagull came in when the Australian Government decided that their Air Force should assist in the hydrographic survey of the Great Barrier Reef. No. 101 (Fleet Co-operation) Flight was formed on 1 July 1925, and six Supermarine Seagull III amphibians were ordered. These machines were essentially Mark IIs with larger radiators, and the first of these was ready by February 1926.

A Seagull II of 440 Flight, off the south coast of Malta. Note the rungs on the rear centre-section strut for access to fuel tanks. (Courtesy of RAF Museum)

By this time, six of the RAF aircraft had served a tour of duty with HMS *Eagle*, but the type had then been pronounced as having 'no potential naval use', particularly because of their habit of porpoising on take-off. They were then confined to coastal (non-carrier) reconnaissance duties and so the type did not come into contention as a future replacement for the long-serving Fairey III series. However, it was given a place in the popular final set piece of the fifth RAF Pageant, where it summoned Flycatchers, followed by Blackburn Darts, to destroy two large replica warships.

In sharp contrast, the Australian Seagulls were used more thoroughly, as their survey work extended into 1927 and continued on northwards to include some 10,000 square miles of Papua New Guinea and one staged flight of 13,000 miles. Referred to by the natives as 'the canoe that goes for up', it was also pronounced a 'delightful' aircraft to fly by one pilot, Commander F.J. Crowther, although in these tropical regions it took more than an hour to reach 8,000ft (but then, a Vickers Victoria transport, at about this time and also in a hot climate, took nearly two hours to reach 10,000ft).

Traditional Supermarine ruggedness was also evident after the survey work was completed, as the Seagulls were assigned to the newly constructed seaplane tender HMAS *Albatross*, commissioned in 1929. As they were not easy to deck land, they were lowered and hoisted aboard but they continued in carrier use until 1933, when their vessel was placed in reserve.

The Seagulls were then transferred to Royal Australian Navy (RAN) cruisers and, in spite of the type's various limitations, three further engineless RAF Seagulls were acquired at the scrap price of £100 each, intended to be used for spares. However, they were found to be in such excellent condition that they were restored to flying condition and put into service use.

By this time, the Seagulls had long lost their appeal for the RAF, but the type continued to occupy the minds of Mitchell's design team even until 1928. Fitting hydro-vanes was considered and various permutations of the hull step position were tried out on N9565 and on N9606.

One aircraft, N9605, was fitted with Handley Page wing slots and a new tail unit with twin fins and rudders. This aircraft, designated Mark IV, was converted to take five passengers in 1929, as the Supermarine Company was looking forward to a small fleet of this later model resuming the old Sea Eagle Southampton–Channel Islands routes. A pilot service was begun in July by the prototype five-passenger conversion (G-AAIZ), but most of August was void owing to serious damage to the hull caused by its hitting a submerged rock. Then, on 2 September, the short-lived business ceased when the aircraft ran into engine trouble.

Two other Seagulls, N9653 and N9654, were converted for civilian use. Registered as G-EBXH and G-EBXI respectively, they began a coastal service at Shoreham, but this also failed owing to inadequate public response.

However, two other modifications of the Seagull were of great significance to Mitchell's team. One was concerned with equipping a Seagull to initiate the testing of catapults for launching aircraft and the second was the exchanging of the usual water-cooled Napier engine for an air-cooled radial engine in a pusher configuration. As we shall see later, when the Seagull V/Walrus appeared, it was as an aircraft engined in this particular way and stressed for catapult launching

AN AMPHIBIAN BOMBER AND AN ENIGMA

While the Mark III Seagull went exclusively to another country, albeit a dominion of the British Empire, one particular design by Mitchell was sold exclusively to a foreign power. This machine was the Scarab, which first flew on 21 May 1924, and was a powerful fighting machine for its period. At this time, there was also a basically similar amphibian, designed for the Admiralty; it was named Sheldrake, and appeared at an air pageant in 1927, but in most respects little is known about it.

The Sheldrake

As early as 1923 the criticisms of the Supermarine Seagull led to an Air Ministry order being placed for an improved version. The resultant aircraft was the Sheldrake, whose flying surfaces were virtually identical to those of the Seagull but which had a more efficient boat-like hull very similar to that of the Sea Eagle, if the passenger cabin were discounted. As the new hull shape was selected in response to one of the RAF's criticisms of the Seagull, it is surprising that the noisy stabilising screens on either side of the engine were still retained, as was the separation of the pilot from the rest of the crew – which, as we have seen, had already been avoided in the Seagull II.

Even more surprising was the apparent inactivity around the Sheldrake. Perhaps contributory factors here were the first flights of the Sea Eagle and the Sea Lion III, producing the first batch of the Seagull IIs, and consideration of the larger flying boats, the Scylla and the Swan. But, for whatever reasons, its only known public appearance is recorded as late as 1927, at the Hamble Air Pageant. By this time, it was an obsolete type, as Cozens said:

The writer especially remembers seeing a Sheldrake at the end of the line of aircraft on show at Hamble. This machine, N180, looked very much like an 'old gaffer' ... but it did have a certain dignity when it took off and was 'attacked' by three Gloster Gamecocks in their silver paint, black and white squares [No. 43 Squadron markings] and RAF roundels.

No production orders were placed for this enigmatic machine.

The Scarab

A year after the Sheldrake prototype was ordered, the second aircraft made its maiden flight – the first of a Spanish requirement for twelve aircraft. There was no prototype for this aircraft and, as it was in a great many respects similar to the Sheldrake, it seems obvious that the Air Ministry order for the earlier aircraft provided most of the design work for the Spanish order – at little extra cost to Supermarine.

King Alfonso XIII of Spain was a frequent visitor to the annual RAF air shows at Hendon and must have gained an early appreciation of the new British 'control without occupation' tactics demonstrated there. Thus it was that, in pursuit of their country's objectives in North Africa, the Spanish Royal Naval Air Service asked Supermarine to produce an amphibian capable of carrying a bomb load of 454 kilos – it having been noticed that the passenger-carrying capacity of the Sea Eagle promised a suitable basis for a design. Supermarine suggested that the plans being drawn for their new Sheldrake would be a more suitable model for the project, especially as Mitchell had been devising improvements with the naval Seagull II, as we have seen.

While the navigator and gunner were still situated behind the wings and out of effective communication with the pilot in the Sheldrake, the Scarab version was built with the three-man crew grouped together in front of the wings. In view of this weight redistribution, the engine was now returned to the more familiar pusher configuration. The gunner was now more aggressively forward facing, just behind the pilot, with the navigator/bomb aimer having a cabin in the hull immediately behind and below his cockpit position.

Mitchell adopted the newer practice of siting the fuel tanks above the fuselage, not only for the benefit of the navigator but also for the stowage of twelve 50lb bombs which could be dropped via a sealable aperture in the bottom of the hull. Four 100lb bombs were also carried under the wings, and the total weight of bombs carried amounted to the equivalent of six men. As the Scarab was designed for a crew of three and had to carry a machine gun, ammunition and a considerable amount of fuel, and as it had the flexibility of an amphibian configuration, it was an attractive single-engined proposition for its buyers.

The first Scarab made its maiden flight on 21 May 1924, but whether all twelve actually saw service is unclear. One of the Scarabs was damaged in acceptance trials when its Spanish pilot hit the side of a Union Castle liner when taking off; and the ship sent to collect them had a cargo lift 4in too small in one dimension, so the machines had to survive a severe Bay of Biscay storm stowed under tarpaulins as deck cargo.

Nevertheless, Scarabs were seen above Barcelona at the 1925 Royal Review of the Spanish forces by King Alfonso, and they equipped a seaplane carrier, the *Dédalo*. This vessel was a converted merchant vessel and lacked a landing deck. The aircraft were lowered into the water or raised from it by crane, like its Seagull predecessor. Based at Carageno and commanded by the king's nephew, the unit took part in actions against Riff and Jibala insurgents in the Spanish Moroccan campaign, including bombing raids in support of an amphibian landing at Al Hoceima.

The Moroccan conflict ended soon afterwards in 1926 and Supermarine publicity ran as follows: 'A large number of these machines have been bought by the Spanish Government, and these have been in operation for the past year in Morocco with the most satisfactory results.'

The first Scarab for the Spanish Royal Naval Air Service. (Courtesy of P. Jarrett)

The Supermarine Company was no doubt mindful of the new RAF tactics of 'control without occupation', but its publicity did not lead to any British orders. The sole Sheldrake was not heard of again, but at least it had paved the way for the significant order from Spain. And it might be noted in passing that the more successful hull-planing configuration developed for the Sheldrake, and also employed on the Scarab, was an important influence upon the eventual Seagull V / Walrus design.

All of these machines continued Mitchell's development of the medium-sized amphibian biplane (of about 46ft in wingspan). Thanks to Mitchell's original Seal, which first flew in May 1921, the financial position of Supermarine began to improve, as the total of thirty-three Seal/Seagull orders were in addition to the small fleet of Sea Eagle passenger amphibians and the twelve Spanish amphibian bombers. It is clear that its chief designer, R.J. Mitchell, was becoming a valuable asset to the company.

MITCHELL'S UGLY DUCKLINGS

During the First World War, Felixstowe F2 and F3 flying boats had been operated successfully on coastal reconnaissance duties despite their various problems, and they were replaced after the Armistice by the F5 from the same makers. However, Flight Lieutenant D'Arcy Greig (later to figure in the Supermarine S5 story) recorded that the latter was no better a performer on water than its predecessors:

> They were grossly underpowered by two Rolls-Royce Eagle VIII engines, and if there happened to be a flat calm at time of take-off, they frequently refused to unstick. On such occasions the pilot had to taxi frenziedly up and down the Solent and around in circles in order to disturb the surface of the water before trying again, but even then they sometimes failed to get airborne.

These flying boats had slab-sided hulls which were prone to leakage and so the Air Ministry was concerned to see if the Linton Hope type of hull, which they regarded as a success on the Pemberton-Billing AD Boat, could be adopted on aircraft of the Felixstowe size. Specifications N3B and N4 had been issued for this purpose, but the slow process of fulfilling this requirement by various manufacturers around the country lasted until well after the war, by which time Supermarine came into contention with the Scylla.

The Scylla

In response to a contract for a five-seat military flying boat, the new machine was conceived in 1923 as a torpedo-carrying triplane with biplane stabilisers, and it was to be powered by two main engines and a much smaller, auxiliary one, sited in the hull to drive a water propeller for taxiing. This last feature seems particularly old-fashioned, looking back to the earlier Pemberton-Billing days of the company and, in particular, the PB 7 (see below).

Why just the hull of the Scylla was completed is unknown, as was its final fate. At this distance in time, one must accept the view of the authors of *Supermarine Aircraft* that, after taxiing trials with the hull, 'the fate of the Scylla design is wrapped in mystery'. Most likely, Mitchell's rapidly developing confidence as a designer was an important factor. As a new contract was received soon afterwards for a large commercial amphibian, his thoughts could turn from the traditional thinking represented by the Scylla to a more forward-looking aircraft, given the confidence that must have followed from his successful Commercial Amphibian design and the small fleet of passenger-carrying Sea Eagles.

This new Air Ministry requirement was for a commercial, twin-engined amphibian and it must have had an immediate appeal, as Supermarine believed that it would be the first of its type in the world. Also, as it was required to carry twelve passengers, it would come out at about the same size as the military Scylla and therefore it might be that the first machine was soon relegated to merely providing information for the more exciting new biplane – which Mitchell would have predicted to be a more efficient aircraft. It could also surely have been easily retro-fitted for the military purposes specified for the Scylla. Certainly the earlier machine seems to have been used only for water taxiing trials, and photographic evidence shows a very basic framework erected on the hull to accommodate (perhaps temporarily) the two engines for these purposes.

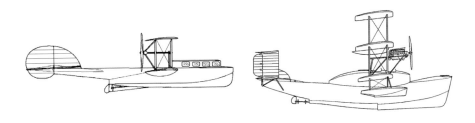

The PB 7.   The Scylla.

The Swan

At least it can be more certainly recorded that when the new machine, to be named the Swan, first appeared in 1924, it was a considerable redesign of the triplane Scylla, being an equal span biplane with a forward-folding wing arrangement like the Sea Eagle of the previous year.

Indeed the Swan might, in some ways, be regarded as a scaled-up Sea Eagle, although doubling the number of passengers to be carried necessitated accommodating them in the main body of the hull rather than in the forward position which had been approvingly commented upon in the earlier aircraft. Again, the fuel tanks were placed high enough to provide gravity feed to the engines, which were situated between the wings, as well as to provide unusually roomy and fume-free accommodation for the passengers. The fin and rudder outlines also resembled those of the Sea Eagle.

However, Mitchell's less complex use of dihedral only on the outer sections of the lower mainplane was new, and the three vertical tail surfaces anticipated his larger designs of the next decade. The single plane stabiliser was also new to larger Supermarine aircraft and was kept well clear of the water by the upward slope of the rear section of the hull. This was very unusual for the time, although not quite an innovation in flying boat design (see the much smaller French Tellier T3 or Latham HB3). Neither was it as graceful as the upward sweep of the future Southampton rear fuselage but, at least, it represented a bold new step in Mitchell hull design, without previous experimentation with smaller hulls.

The decision to employ three fins had also led to a reversal of the chief designer's earlier practice, from the Commercial Amphibian onwards, whereby the tailplane had been supported by the fin, with the aid of a complex arrangement of struts. The new feature, with the tailplane supporting the fins, also anticipated most of Mitchell's later seaplanes and was a more elegant

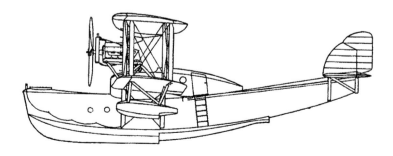

The Swan.

configuration than the backward-looking biplane tail approach proposed for the Scylla.

On the other hand, the upswept fuselage and the boat-like prow, which was flared outwards at the top to counteract spray, were features in common with the earlier machine, as they had presumably been proven to be effective by its taxiing trials. The raised cockpit superstructure was also very reminiscent of the unfinished Scylla, and it contributed significantly to the clumsiness of the hull profile. Cozens' comments are complementary, if not always complimentary:

> The Swan had several features which showed improvements on previous designs, and no doubt these led to its success. The keel had an upward curve towards the tail that enabled it to take off more readily and this feature was noticeable in all later flying boat hulls built throughout the flying boat era, even to the Saunders-Roe Princess of the nineteen fifties …

An informal moment in the royal visit showing the impressive size of the Swan, including the substantial samson post at the prow. Mitchell is to the right of the Prince of Wales. (Courtesy of *The Sentinel*, Stoke-on-Trent)

The struts of the Swan's centre-section formed large W's which made for great strength and the large fins and rudders and the considerable spacing between the wings made this aircraft a success from a handling point of view. At any rate, Captain Biard was pleased and so was the Air Ministry, but no one could say that the Swan was a handsome machine with its rounded bow and strange looking cabin and the pilot's cockpit at the top.

The 'strange looking cabin', which housed a crew of two, sat on the top of the main fuselage so as not to interfere with the passenger space and, as the proposed passenger windows had yet not been fitted, the offending side-view was unrelieved. The same had been true of the Scylla and, while Supermarine had no doubt chosen the latter's name to suit its proposed military role, it might seem to others that the name reflected its stark appearance – according to Ovid, the beautiful Scylla was turned into a thing of terror and, in Homer, Odysseus manages to sail past the monster but not before she catches and devours six of his men. As the new design was to have a more pacific role, the new aircraft was named Swan although, despite its size, 'ugly duckling' comes more to mind.

Be that as it may, the new aircraft was first flown by Biard on 25 March 1924 and, at this time, displayed the triangular cut-outs in the leading edges of the wings to enable them to fold forward. The Swan also had the sort of retracting undercarriage arrangement that Mitchell had designed for his single-engined amphibians, but the much increased size of the new machine necessitated the novelty of some form of servo assistance. Biard described the mechanism as follows:

It would have been quite impossible to wind down the six-foot wheels and powerful landing-carriage, which had to stand the weight of several tons of aircraft and passengers! So a neat device was fitted to the machine to do the work quickly and efficiently for us. This consisted of a small propeller, which, when not in use, was set sideways to the direction in which we were flying. When we wanted to lower the landing gear, this propeller was swung round to face the direction of our course, and the whirling propeller was connected by cogs to a handle which wound very rapidly round and lowered the wheels into place; by turning the propeller rearward the wheels were wound up out of our way under the wings, and the machine was then able to descend on water. This gear, after one or two adjustments following minor troubles during tests, when the Swan behaved neither like fish, flesh, nor fowl, proved remarkably efficient, and wound the heavy landing gear into place in about half a minute or less.

Biard also describes the visit of the Prince of Wales to Supermarine, and to the Swan in particular, on 27 June in the same year. On being invited to climb the 10ft steel ladder to the cabins (see drawing on p.73), he declined because of his dress sword.

By the time of the prince's visit, the Swan's two 360hp Rolls-Royce Eagle engines had been replaced by Napier Lion engines, each developing 90hp more than the Rolls-Royce units, thereby increasing the Swan's top speed by 13mph. The folding of the wings and the leading-edge cut-outs had also been dispensed with. Plans for an RAF version of the Swan were also being actively pursued at this time – which may have had some influence on the change to the fixed-wing layout and possibly throws more light upon the decision to terminate the development of the military Scylla.

Meanwhile, the first of the N4 specification aircraft, the Fairey Atalanta, had made its maiden flight, but its 139ft wingspan and four 650hp Rolls-Royce Condor engines made it a less attractive proposition for the drastically reduced post-war services. In comparison, the Swan had only half the wingspan, two smaller engines and yet was only 10mph slower; it also embodied the Linton Hope type of hull in which the Air Ministry was interested.

Successful trials of the Swan at the Marine Aircraft Experimental Establishment, Felixstowe, followed which were to have important results for the fortunes of Supermarine. On its return to Supermarine, it was now fitted out for its passenger-carrying role. Company publicity pointed out that the machine was not only the first twin-engined commercial amphibian but that the provided accommodation set new standards:

> This is the first twin-engined amphibian flying boat to be built in the world and it may also be fairly claimed to be the first twin-engined commercial flying boat.
>
> An important feature of this machine is that the whole of the hull is devoted to passenger accommodation. There are no internal obstructions of any kind, and the amount of room in the saloon far exceeds that of any commercial land plane. The internal accommodation consists of one large passenger saloon, elaborately furnished and upholstered and with every comfort. Forward of the saloon is the luggage compartment, fitted with racks for the stowage of passenger baggage. Aft of the saloon is the buffet, with all necessary fittings to supply light refreshment during the journey. Still further aft are the lavatories, which are efficiently and fully equipped.

As such, it was registered as G-EBJY and first flew on 9 June 1926, carrying a representative of the newly formed Imperial Airways and eight excited female employees of the company among its passengers. A slight reduction in passenger seating further allowed Supermarine to set new standards in passenger accommodation, which Biard fully confirmed: 'the Swan, then the world's largest amphibian … was a real cabin-liner of the air, with comfortable armchairs, big porthole windows, a commodious passage along the centre of the living accommodation, and all sorts of luxuries and refinements which were very new to aircraft at that time'.

A more neutral observer from the *Aeroplane* agreed, saying that 'the appointments are exquisite' with 'a commodious passenger saloon padded luxuriously and in which there are ten cosy armchairs. An ample porthole is provided for each chair.'

Cozens describes a later, and more mundane use for the passenger compartment in the course of his recollections of this aircraft:

> Both Rolls-Royce Eagles and Napier Lions were tried but the Lions were finally chosen. The writer recalls this machine when it was used in the colours of Imperial Airways as a freighter to bring bags of early potatoes and boxes of daffodils from the Channel Islands. The large mid-section made this possible and highly suitable for bulky cargoes. I remember seeing the horse drawn market carts down on the slipway being loaded from the Swan.

The aircraft had been loaned by the Air Ministry to Imperial Airways in order to supplement the service of Supermarine's remaining two smaller sisters, the Sea Eagles, on their Channel Islands service. It operated during 1926 and 1927 but, as the *Guernsey Evening Press* reported, 'during the normal rigorous inspection prior to leaving Southampton on 12 April, a structural defect was discovered which necessitated the stripping of the whole machine'. As a result, the Swan was scrapped.

The Swan, later, without wing cut-outs or undercarriage. (Courtesy of E.B. Morgan)

Imperial Airways' next long-distance seaplane was not to be the Swan, how-ever, and so the machine's main significance remained that of providing the prototype for the Royal Air Force's next standard maritime reconnaissance air-craft, the far more attractive Supermarine Southampton of 1925.

(For the sake of completeness, it ought to be mentioned that, at this very time, Mitchell was also required to design his first land plane, the Sparrow I. In complete contrast to the bulky Swan and even the medium-sized Scarabs, it had a mere 34ft wingspan and was designed to compete in an Air Ministry light aircraft competition. Owing to the poor performance of the engine fitted, it was unsuccessful. In the following year, 1925, as Sparrow II, it was configured as a parasol monoplane to test the effectiveness of wings with dif-ferent aerofoils.)

4

ANNUS MIRABILIS

DESIGNING THE NAVY'S STANDARD RECONNAISSANCE MACHINE

It is surely no exaggeration to identify 1925 as the year when two of Mitchell's aircraft stood out dramatically from what had preceded them. While he had had early successes, incrementally improving on conventional machines, this year marked his full emergence as a designer who had transcended the design conventions that he had inherited and who was now striking out boldly into the future.

The young man who had joined his aero firm in 1916 at the age of 21, assisting with the designs of others, nine years later produced the first standard naval reconnaissance aircraft since the end of the First World War and the racing floatplane that set the basic design configuration for all subsequent Schneider Trophy machines.

By this time, the need to find a suitable replacement for the Felixstowe military flying boats was becoming critical, let alone the possibility of creating aerial links with the outposts of Empire – as the Secretary of State for Air, Sir Samuel Hoare, recorded: 'In 1922, there were no aeroplanes capable of maintaining a long-distance service. The existing heavier-than-air machines were low-powered, very noisy and uncomfortable. Flying boats had almost ceased to exist and there was no plan for an Empire air line of any kind.'

And the first responses to the Admiralty specification for a flying boat to replace the Felixstowe machines were not such attractive propositions in terms of design or in the post-war 'anti-waste' climate. The Fairey Atalanta, which had made its maiden flight in 1923, had a 139ft wingspan and four 650hp Rolls-Royce Condor engines; the English Electric P5 Kingston, which flew in the following year, was essentially a continuation of the old N3 specification of 1917; and the Short S2 of the same year, while being forward-looking because of its metal hull, utilised the old F3 flying surfaces.

In view of this unsatisfactory situation, the Air Ministry authorised, also in 1924, the building of six airships initially to provide a service to Egypt, but the project became an embarrassment because of many delays. The success of the trials of the more compact, twin-engined Swan was very welcome news to the Air Ministry officials, who had previously been very impressed by the standards set by the Sea Eagle in 1923. Their appreciation of the new standards in flying boat performance now being established by Mitchell led to the very unusual step of ordering (no doubt with considerable relief) straight off the drawing board a reconnaissance flying boat based on the Swan amphibian passenger carrier. It was fortunate for Supermarine that the Estimates of January had, at the expense of those for the navy and for the army, provided for an increase of £2.5 million for the RAF.

PREVIOUS: Southampton Mark IIs. (From a painting by the author)

The Southampton

Supermarine received specification R18/24 in the August of 1924, for a modified and slightly enlarged Swan type flying boat, and Mitchell's main response was to have the Swan hull lines redrawn to improve its streamlining.

Although the new machine continued the planing configuration that Mitchell had been developing since 1923 with the Sea Eagle, it now became a part of one of the most elegant hulls that Mitchell had ever been responsible for. Indeed, the transformation of the lines of its prototype, the Swan, was dramatic. The more utilitarian requirements of a military machine allowed the removal of the ad hoc looking, high-drag crew compartment above the Swan's lower wing and for the passenger baggage compartment to be utilised for the pilot and navigator, seated in tandem in open cockpits. He also streamlined the Swan nose and dramatically upswept the rear of the hull to keep the tail unit well clear of the water (see photograph overleaf).

While this upsweep had been seen earlier on both the small FBA and the Latham Schneider aircraft, as well as on the First World War Grigoravich machines, its incorporation in the much larger Southampton hull was a novel and bold move – of which Mitchell must have been aware, as a 1924 patent on behalf of himself and Supermarine draws explicit attention to the fact that 'the hull is curved upwardly and rearwardly'.

Elsewhere, in larger hull designs, Curtiss and Sikorsky moved from the previous Felixstowe unswept approach to the employment of 'canoe' type hulls with the empennage attached by booms subtended from the wings and supported by girders from the hull.

In contrast, the elegance of Mitchell's sweeping lines was emphasised and complemented by the redesign of the Swan fins, which were now swept back in a single curve, resulting in the new Southampton being regarded as 'probably the most beautiful biplane flying boat that had ever been built' and 'certainly the most beautiful hull ever built'.

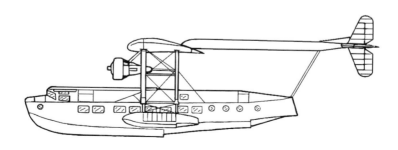

The Sikorsky S-40.

The first Southampton flying boat.

Cozens gives some interesting contemporary information, particularly about the construction of the Southampton hull:

Many considered the Southampton's wooden hull to be the ultimate in design and craftsmanship, in its shape and purpose Mitchell combined his experience in building with Captain Biard's reports on flying and this was recognised by the people of Southampton who subscribed and had a silver shield with the Southampton coat of arms fixed to the bow of N9896.

It was about this time that Scott-Paine and his co-director Commander Bird had a tremendous quarrel which ended with Scott-Paine leaving Supermarine with a fortune which he used to begin the British Power Boat Company at the old boat sheds at Hythe, where the May, Harden and May company built the Felixstowe flying boats of the Great War period.

The late Mr Conrad Mann, who worked on the wooden Southamptons, told me they were built bottom side up so that the two steps and the curved keel, which had been a feature of the Swan, could be built. He said there were six men and two apprentices on each hull and the contract price agreed by them for each hull was £483 19s 4d, so that the money worked out as follows:

Contract price for 6 men to build 1 hull   £483 19s 4d
Wages for 6 men to build 1 hull   £357 19s 4d
Balance   £126

This was shared among the men giving each £21

The two apprentices were paid by the company.

This arrangement seemed to work very well, giving both the management and the men every encouragement to build the machines as quickly as possible, and most of the men bought their bicycles with the lump sum bonus …

Extracts from letters about the Supermarine Southampton which appeared in the *Southern Evening Echo*:

'Southampton people had good cause to remember and honour that machine because it brought a good deal of prestige and a steady flow of work to the factory where it was built.'

This was the time of the Depression and the General Strike, when a machine was finished there was an order for another one. With a steady wage and the prospect of another bonus, the workforce was fortunate and happy. This air of well-being, stimulated by the success of the Schneider Trophy Races, made the firm, and Woolston generally, a vigorous and active area.

About 20 [twenty-four, in fact] of the wooden flying boats were made and, as there was not enough floor space at Woolston, the main components were put on barges and ferried across to the boatsheds at Hythe for assembly. There were often three or four machines moored on the Hythe buoys, their varnished hulls and white wings making a picture that those who saw them would never forget.

This was brought to mind when a Group Captain who saw the picture of the wooden Southampton in the *Echo* remembered his early days on Flight 48[0], an RAF conversion flight stationed at Calshot to train pilots to fly Southamptons, looked in his logbook and found that he had flown that same machine in about 1928. He said that one day a second pilot wanted to change into the first pilot's seat and left his own seat and went to the one behind him, passing between the two propellers … At the nearest point the two propellers were only 9in apart!

Cozens mentions several times the importance of Biard's advice to Mitchell during these early years, and this would have been especially important to Mitchell when there was little theory to guide designers. As Cozens was a neighbour of the test pilot, it would seem very likely that he heard of particular instances where advice was given – and listened to willingly (see Chapter 1).

No doubt the new machine's ability to maintain height on one engine, as well as its maximum range of 500 miles, was more important in Air Ministry minds than any aesthetic considerations. Additionally, there was the extreme practicality of the design. Warren girders (as with the Swan) supported the centre section of the wings without the need for wire bracing, thus enabling a change of engine or servicing to take place unimpeded and without interference to the airframe. This centre-section was plywood covered, again for ease of movement by mechanics, and the leading edges of the outer wing panels were also sheeted for a smoother aerodynamic entry.

It is also notable that the lower wings were not joined to the boat hull, as might be expected; instead, the wing superstructure had attachment points on the top of the hull (see photograph on p.194) and was stabilised laterally by struts from reinforced frames in the hull. In this way, Mitchell retained as much flexibility as possible in the Linton Hope type hull and avoided the cracking around the wing fixing position, experienced at this position by other companies' designs.

In the Swan, this fuselage structure had provided unusually good passenger space for the time and, in the Southampton, it enabled particularly good communication between crew members. Ahead of the pilot was a cockpit for a gunner and, a little further back from where the Swan pilot had been situated, were two staggered positions for rear gunners, one on each side of the centre line. Basic cooking, lavatory and sleeping facilities were also provided, so beginning the provision for equipping the RAF with naval aircraft that could be generally self-sufficient for reasonable periods of time. The siting of petrol tanks in the upper wing centre-section, which Mitchell had established with the Seagull II, was a contributory factor to the improvement to crew conditions, as well as giving a reliable gravity feed to the engines.

The extent of the modifications to the original design were such that a completely new name was considered more appropriate than, say, 'Swan Mark II'. Since the Swan was built as a commercial aircraft, it had not been subject to the 'Aircraft Nomenclature Committee', which required the names of water fowl for small multi-seat amphibians and names of 'seaboard British towns' for larger seaplanes. 'Southampton' was chosen, albeit an estuary port not a seaboard town.

In negotiating this name, the company was now proclaiming Supermarine's increasing status in the community whose dignitaries had welcomed the return of the company's 1922 Schneider Trophy winner from Naples. Cozens' information that a silver shield with the Southampton coat of arms was fixed to the bow of N9896, the first of the batch, can be confirmed in the preceding photograph.

Supermarine thus marked the firm's increasing importance in the industrial community of the area, particularly in view of the Air Ministry order, substantial by the criteria of the day, for six standard military aircraft (N9896–N9901) and an experimental one, N218, to be fitted with a metal hull. These aircraft were also the largest production machines yet to come from Supermarine – the Seagulls and Scarabs had had a wingspan of 46ft, whereas the Southampton spanned 75ft (6ft 4in more than the Swan).

Air Ministry officials must surely have been impressed by the promptness of the delivery of the first of the Southamptons, as Supermarine recorded:

Something of a record in design and construction was achieved with the first machine of this class, for it was designed and built in seven months, was flown for the first time one day and delivered by air from Southampton to the RAF at Felixstowe the next day [11 March 1925].

Three Southamptons over Southampton Docks (with the *Mauretania* in the foreground) and about to overfly the River Itchen and the Supermarine factory at Woolston. (Courtesy of RAF Museum)

Nor could its reputation have been harmed when, after sustaining damage there in a collision with a breakwater, it was taxied by sea all the way back to Woolston for repairs. Pilots thereafter reported that it 'never gave the slightest trouble ... and was a joy to fly'; it was 'a great step forward, a delight to fly and operate' – summed up by Penrose when he reported for the year 1925 that 'it was the beautiful new Supermarine Southampton flying boat which was receiving unstinting approbation from RAF pilots'.

As soon as deliveries to No. 480 Coastal Reconnaissance Flight began, the RAF undertook a series of long-range proving flights. N9896 made a three-day round trip from Felixstowe to Rosyth in Scotland, followed by a fourteen-day exercise with the Scilly Isles as a base, and then a week's cruise around coastal waters; also, four Southamptons covered 10,000 miles in a twenty-day cruise around the British Isles, including exercises with the Royal Navy in the Irish Sea.

These flights established a new standard in naval reconnaissance aircraft. They also marked the point at which Supermarine achieved real economic stability and prosperity. Supermarine publicity pointed out features likely to appeal to potential customers – its ruggedness and the many practicalities of its design – and went on to describe features which the RAF had proved:

The machine has been flown continually on one engine, and can be manoeuvred and turned against the pull of the one engine without difficulty. The well-known qualities of the Napier 'Lion' engine have been used to the

A Southampton II, the sixth of the 1929 Argentinian batch of eight. (Courtesy of Solent Sky Museum)

fullest extent by an efficient installation, with the result that not the slightest troubles have been experienced from the power units throughout the many thousands of hours of flying these machines have carried out.

Mention was also made of the metal hull version of the Southampton that had been ordered by the Air Ministry – which gave rise to the Southampton II appearing in 1926. As a result, the total order for the type eventually rose to eighty-three, when the metal-hulled Marks II to IV were ordered and when sales were extended to Japan, Argentina and Turkey.

The Royal Air Force Far East Flight

The new Mark II machine also encouraged the Air Ministry, in 1926, to order four new Southamptons, with increased petrol and oil capacities and with larger radiators, specifically to initiate a proving cruise to the far reaches of the Empire. As the Secretary of State for Air put it, 'it was our settled policy to show the Air Force, as the Navy showed the Fleet, in the distant parts of the Empire'.

The confidence in the Supermarine machine is evident from the fact that the cruise, by essentially standard RAF machines, was to incorporate overflights of many countries only previously visited by the pioneering Cobham, and to go as far as Australia, which had only been visited, singly, by four previous aeroplanes. Additionally, it was to circumnavigate that continent – a feat which had been achieved only once to that date, by a Fairey IIID on 6–18 May 1924.

Readers of the 1927 issue of *Jane's* would, therefore, have been well aware of the ambition and confidence of Supermarine when the company announced:

A number of the metal-hulled 'Southamptons' are now being completed to equip the RAF Far East Flight. These Southamptons will be flown out to India, via the Mediterranean, and then on to Singapore and along the Dutch East Indies to Australia, where an extended flight round the Australian sea-board, in conjunction with the Royal Australian Air Force, is contemplated.

The leader of an earlier Mediterranean flight of the Southampton I, Squadron Leader Livock, was again chosen, as well as Flight Lieutenant H.G. Sawyer, who, as a junior officer, had taken part in one of the early British Isles proving flights. But, on the occasion of this much more extensive and important Far East Flight, a Group Captain was put in command – H.M. Cave-Brown-Cave (who, on arrival in Australia, became known as 'Home-Sweet-Home'). His orders were 'to open the air route to Australia and the East, to select landing sites, to see how far flying boats and their crews were capable of operating away from fixed bases and under widely varying climatic conditions, and to show the flag'.

Thus, while there was a clear imperialist motive behind the proposed flight, the other main concern was to prove the feasibility of reliable air transport, with scheduled stops for servicing and for inspections to see how the aircraft were standing up to the testing itinerary.

The main cruise began from Plymouth on 17 October 1927, and finished at Seletar, Singapore, on 28 February 1928. The engines were replaced on arrival at Singapore and one of the aircraft, as prearranged, was dismantled and sent back to England for detailed inspection. The flight then proceeded to circumnavigate Australia, and fly around the China Sea to Hong Kong and back. In all, they flew 27,000 miles, in formation, at an average speed of 80mph and in sixty-two timetabled stages of about 400 miles at a time. During the whole cruise, the Southamptons only fell behind schedule three times, twice because of bad weather and once with engine trouble; one machine was delayed by a cracked airscrew boss.

Another extended formation flight carried out by Mitchell's aircraft, the Baltic flight, included the cities of Esbjerg, Copenhagen, Stockholm, Helsinki, Tallin, Riga, Memel, Gothenburg and Oslo. A total distance of over 3,000 miles was covered, again without mishap. Squadron Leader Livock, who was second in command of the Far East Flight and leader of the formation, gives a full account of these flights in his autobiography, *To the Ends of the Air*, which is well worth reading for its accounts of the difficulties and frustrations encountered when pioneering air routes in areas where, understandably, there was little comprehension of aviators' special needs.

Southamptons of 201 Squadron during the 1930 Baltic flight. (Courtesy of E.B. Morgan)

Two out of a flight of four Douglas DCWs had flown round the world during 1924, and other nations made more publicised formation flights in following years. Yet the Southamptons' Far East Cruise in particular, which was completed in scheduled stages by the entire formation, must be regarded as directly instrumental in the establishment of the Imperial Airways Empire routes of the 1930s, and as one of the milestones in aviation history. The *Daily Mail* was in no doubt: 'As a demonstration of reliability, the flight will rank as one of the greatest feats in the history of aviation.'

Another assessment of Mitchell's achievement in the field of seaplane design appeared in the caption to a picture of a Southampton I flying boat featured at the beginning of *Jane's* for 1925: 'One of the most notable successes in post-war aircraft design.' It was surely no coincidence that the Supermarine entry in *Jane's* for the same year records, for the first time, the identity of its chief designer: 'The firm has a very large design department continually employed on new designs, under the chief designer and engineer, R.J. Mitchell, who has established himself as one of the leading flying boat and amphibian designers in the country.'

He had just passed his 30th birthday.

THE REVOLUTIONARY SCHNEIDER FLOATPLANE

After Supermarine's resounding defeat in the 1923 Schneider Trophy competition, funding and support for future competitions was now made available by the Air Ministry. This allowed Mitchell the luxury of designing an aircraft that

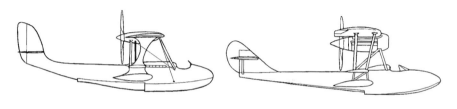

Sea Urchin.   Savoia S.51.

was not dependent on straitened company resources and recycled airframes, and it turned out to be a significant departure from all the Supermarine aircraft which had preceded it.

As with the Spitfire, however, his immediate response was not especially original. Indeed, his initial proposal, the 'Sea Urchin', still looked towards the flying boat approach, and might be regarded as essentially an improvement on the Italian Savoia S.51 racer, whose 1922 speed record for seaplanes (174.08mph) had been only marginally less than the top speed of the later Supermarine Sea Lion III. Nevertheless, Mitchell proposed a sesquiplane configuration similar to that of the Italian design and with a similar high thrust line. On the other hand, it might be noted that his hull revealed somewhat similar styling to that of his Southampton, particularly in respect of the upswept rear hull. Additionally, the drag penalty of the high-mounted engine was to be reduced by situating the engine in the hull and driving the propeller through bevel-geared shafting – some response, at least, to the successful American in-line engined CR-3.

The Sea Urchin proposal was not pursued because of serious doubts about the practicality of the propeller shaft gearing and, fortunately, the American hosts for the 1924 event sportingly postponed the competition as none of the other nations who were expected to compete were sufficiently prepared. As the American winner of the last Schneider Trophy contest achieved an average speed 20mph more than Mitchell's modified Sea Lion III, a comprehensively different design had really been called for and Mitchell now had time to produce such an airframe.

The allocated Air Ministry serial number for the new machine was N197, although this was never carried, and despite what turned out to be a revolutionary design Supermarine referred to the new machine only as the S4 – 'S' presumably referring to Schneider and '4' indicating that it was the successor of the Mark III Sea Lion.

The S.4

When the secrecy surrounding its build was lifted, its sensational appearance was well summed up by *Flight*:

One may describe the Supermarine Napier S.4 as having been designed in an inspired moment. That the design is bold no one will deny, and the greatest credit is due to R.J. Mitchell for his courage in striking out on entirely new lines. It is little short of astonishing that he should have been able to break away from the types with which he had been connected, and not only abandon the flying boat type in favour of a twin float arrangement, but actually change from braced biplane to the pure cantilever wing of the S.4.

The dramatic leap from the type of aircraft he had modified for the previous two trophy competitions can be readily appreciated from the opposite side views.

It ought to be noted that nearly a year earlier the French speed record holder, the Bernard V-2 land plane, had displayed some features which might have prompted Mitchell's design. Its Hispano-Suiza engine was a broad arrow design similar to that of the S4's Napier Lion engine and it was faired almost identically into the fuselage and wings; it also had cantilever flying surfaces, underwing radiators and a similar pilot's cockpit position.

Nevertheless, when Penrose later wrote of 'the startlingly novel and beautiful Supermarine S4', he was at least reflecting the dramatic appearance of a revolutionary floatplane design and was surely right in responding to its fine lines. In comparison, it might not be unduly partisan to consider that the Bernard land plane had a much more clumsy appearance.

Supermarine's Alan Clifton gave a more clinical 'in-house' response and singled out the unique attachment of the floats: 'It was an exceptionally clean design, with a central skeleton of steel tubing which included daring cantilevered float struts.' This 'central skeleton' consisted of two sturdy 'A' frames, with the engine mounting bolted to the front frame and the rear fuselage section fixed to the rear one; between these two frames, the wing centre-section was positioned. The floats were attached to the feet of the frames, carefully faired into the tops of the floats, with similar fairings at the fuselage join. This characteristically and deceptively simple arrangement of the frames was known in the works, less reverently, as 'the clothes horse'.

Perhaps because approval to begin building had only been received on 18 March 1925, and also because of this move from flying boat building, Supermarine subcontracted provision of the floats to Shorts, whose own testing tank had been specifically built for simulating aircraft conditions. As the cantilever wing proposal represented a bold departure from the earlier wire-braced company types – and, indeed, from almost all other aircraft of the time – stringers were rebated into the ribs and an early form of stressed skinning was achieved by sheeting the wing, top and bottom, with load-bearing plywood which decreased in thickness towards the tips.

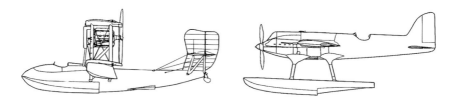

The Sea Lion II (1922).   The S4 (1925).

Thus it was that Mitchell felt able to take the radical step of dispensing with struts and wire bracings for the wings and tail surfaces. He also did away with bracing wires for the floats, although they were fitted with two thin-section cross members. An appreciation of the conceptual leap represented by the S4 can be gained by a comparison of its forward-looking cantilevered structure with that of the previous Sea Lion, which had thirty-three struts and forty-two bracing or external control wires.

With the new machine, the control surfaces were activated from within the structure via rods and torque tubes, and streamlining was also achieved by mounting the newer Lamblin radiators horizontally on the underside of the wings – their fins and the oil-cooling pipes on the underside of the fuselage were the only significant protuberances on the whole machine, with the coolant being carried to and from the engine via piping buried in the underside of the wings.

The following reminiscence of Cozens reminds one that the S4, despite its futuristic shape and polished metal cowlings, was built with traditional woodworking techniques. Its sound, however, was something else – no doubt the result of its ungeared racing engine, producing propeller tip speeds around the speed of sound (2,600rpm turning an 8ft 6in airscrew – go figure):

> After being beaten in 1923 by trying to make the best of an outdated machine, Mitchell went to the other extreme and produced something that was far ahead of its time. It was, of course, of wooden construction, not surprising as neither the designers nor the workforce were capable of building a sophisticated metal machine, and [the fuselage] exploited the Linton Hope technique to the limit … It was built in great secrecy which gave rise to even more curiosity and expectancy than was usual for a Schneider Trophy, always a sensitive subject and it was guarded like a racehorse in a training stables.
>
> By raising the compression ratio the Napier's power was increased and the metal Fairey Reed propeller was quite new in design and construction, so that when it finally emerged and the engine was run up a new sound came,

something that the local people had never heard before, and indeed, very few people ever heard in all their life, a sort of high pitched scream of immense power.

Radiator drag was reduced to a minimum by building it flush into the wings, and because it was made of thin copper plates soldered together it had to be very carefully formed and fitted …

Plainly, this aeroplane needed very skilful handling, more so because the mid-wing shape made visibility poor, and Captain Biard was the only man who could fly it, and an eyewitness said that even he made an airborne hop of a mile before he finally got off between Lee-on-Solent and Calshot …

Apart from the mid-wing configuration, the pilot also had limited vision on account of being situated low down; Biard claimed to have nearly collided with the liner *Majestic* on take-off – having not seen it at all until the last minute – and, when he came to land, he nearly hit a dredger. However, having survived the traumas of the first flight, the new machine went on to gain the world speed record for seaplanes and the outright British Speed Record: 226.75mph – nearly 40mph more than the Curtiss CR-3 record established the previous October.

When the S4 team arrived at Chesapeake Bay, near Baltimore, for the forthcoming Schneider Trophy competition, the tented accommodation for the aircraft and for the workshops was found not to be ready. Having arrived on 5 October, it was only possible to begin erecting the aircraft on 12 October, and days then elapsed before weather conditions allowed test flying to begin. Then Biard went down with influenza and a gale caused tents to collapse. A heavy pole fell across the tail unit of the S4, which was only repaired in time for the navigation tests on the 23rd of the month. By this time, Biard was up and about and insisted on flying the S4 as only he had had experience of handling this revolutionary machine.

Unfortunately, the S4 story was not to have a *Boys' Own* ending, as it crashed into the bay following a steep turn which appeared, perhaps, to have been caused by 'flutter'; a high-speed stall or wing distortion was also suggested by contemporary observers. Whatever the cause, it luckily occurred at low level and Biard survived. Mitchell, always concerned for the safety of his pilots, had set out to rescue him but his boat had engine failure. Biard was picked up after some time in very cold water. His own account of the accident was that, as he came out of a turn at speed and dived down for a straight run, the control stick set up such violent side-to-side oscillations that he lost control.

The phenomenon of flutter was being experienced at about this time with military aircraft. Penrose quotes Flight Lieutenant Linton Ragg of the Royal Aircraft Establishment at Farnborough as experiencing similar stick behaviour:

'wing flutter had caused trying experiences, such as coming down with hand and knees badly bruised by the control column as it played hide-and-seek round the cockpit'. Biard's description of similar side-to-side movement of the control column points to aileron flutter, and later remarks at Supermarine confirm this conclusion: Mitchell, later concerned about the need to avoid overbalancing of the Spitfire ailerons in a dive, wrote somewhat enigmatically, 'I believe this is the cause of several accidents involving ailerons', and Ernest Mansbridge, explaining the thickness of the preceding Type 224 wing being due to caution, was more direct, 'We were still very concerned about possible flutter, having encountered that with the S4 seaplane'.

Major John Buchanan, who had represented the technical department of the Air Ministry at the competition, merely reported that the S4 had stalled, although he may have suspected 'pilot error' (such as unfamiliarity with high speed stalling). His recommendations for future responses to Schneider Trophy competitions included the employment of pilots specially trained for high speed flight – as per the American Navy and Army teams of the last two contest wins.

While civilian pilots had abundant skill and were willing to risk the dangers of competition flying, their usual flying experience was in much slower machines. The case of Henri Biard was not untypical. The S4 was first flown by him on 25 August and, despite reporting slight wing tremors, he had to leave soon afterwards for the Schneider competition in America. When he resumed flying,

Mitchell (centre left) in front of the completed S4. Biard is third from right.
(Courtesy of Solent Sky Museum)

The S4 on approach.

influenza and damage to the floatplane resulted in its only just being ready for the trophy navigability trials on 23 October. Not only had his experience on the revolutionary S4 been very limited but, between his flying the Sea Lion III at a maximum speed of 175mph in 1923 and achieving 239mph in the new machine two years later, his day-to-day flying experience with Supermarine was with the Swan passenger amphibian, the Scarab reconnaissance amphibian, the Sparrow I light land plane, and the Southampton I flying boat, whose top speeds averaged out at something less than 100mph.

While the American phase of the Schneider Trophy competitions had brought no luck to Supermarine, it can be seen as a most important milestone in Mitchell's career. The S4 was to set the design pattern for all future Schneider Trophy aircraft, and its clean cantilever flying surfaces were to be echoed by similar silhouettes in the none-too-distant Second World War.

Later, when Mitchell returned to the design of racing floatplanes, he turned from the wooden airframe of this 1925 aircraft to employ the metal structures that were also to become a feature of the future generations of fighter aircraft. It was his successes in the next three Schneider Trophy competitions that established his reputation outside the aircraft industry. But, when one considers the quantum shift from the Sea Lion of 1922 to the S4 of 1925, and the precedent that this latter aircraft set for the future, a special place should be reserved in British aviation history, and in Mitchell's design career, for the ill-fated but beautiful S4. As E. Bazzocchi, of Aeronautica Macchi, said, 'the real revolution of 1925 was the appearance of the Supermarine S4: its very clean design set the pattern for all subsequent Schneider racers'.

The S4 was a failure, but it had marked the emergence of a notably innovative designer dramatically pushing forward the frontiers of high speed flight. Indeed, Supermarine's publicity in 1926 points out that the previously quoted top speed of over 226mph was later increased to an impressive 239mph.

⑤

SCHNEIDER TROPHY SUCCESSES

THE HIGH SPEED DESIGNER CONFIRMED

After the failure of the revolutionary S4 in the 1925 Schneider Trophy, success in events not long afterwards led the shy young man who had joined his firm at the age of 21 to be honoured at Buckingham Palace, to give a talk on the BBC and to be elected a Fellow of the Royal Aeronautical Society. His solid, everyday work with Supermarine's various amphibians and flying boats did not place his name in front of the general public; his involvement with the Schneider Trophy events of 1927–1931, however, was another matter.

The Schneider Trophy had begun in 1913 as a contest between the aero clubs of various nations, most of whose members were enthusiastic amateurs, as were their pilots. While the trophy continued to be organised by the clubs, the character and costs of the meetings had, by 1926, produced the first confrontation of government subsidised teams with well-organised military pilots and support staff. Equally, the demands of producing the sophisticated technology required of the modern winning entry was evidenced by the non-showing of Britain in that year, and by the complete or partial failure of all the leading aircraft which did compete, owing to lack of adequate development time.

While government assistance for a British entry had already been in evidence in 1925, increased support thereafter prompted *Flight* to comment that 'Never in the history of British aviation have we tackled an international speed race in so thorough a manner.' Mitchell was now able to profit from this even more determined support in the next two competitions, mainly thanks to Air Vice-Marshall W.G.H. Salmond, the Air Member for Supply & Research at the Air Ministry, and the Secretary for State for Air, Sir Samuel Hoare, allocating funds from the existing Air Ministry development budget.

Work was soon under way, involving careful appraisal by wind tunnel and tank testing of quarter scale models. Particular attention was to be paid to floats, flush-wing radiators and airscrews. Gloster, Supermarine and Shorts were asked to design machines capable of speeds not less than 265mph at 1,000ft, and Napier was responding by increasing the Lion engine's compression ratio to 10:1, with a view to approaching the 900hp mark.

Faith in this reliable engine was justified when it did, in fact, deliver 900hp in the ungeared version and 875hp in a geared one. Just as metal propellers were found to be superior to wooden ones as tip speeds increased, so it was considered that any extra weight or loss of engine rpm because of reduction gearing would be well offset by greater propeller efficiency.

PREVIOUS: The Supermarine S6B winning the 1931 Schneider Trophy. (From a painting by the author)

In this respect, when the Air Ministry accepted the proposals of Supermarine, Gloster and Shorts, they were not only departing from the previous American and current Italian concentration of effort on one aircraft type, but were clearly further hedging their bets by supporting two Supermarine entries with geared engines and one with an ungeared unit, a geared Gloster machine and two ungeared ones, as well as a Short seaplane powered by a more standard air-cooled radial engine. This last aircraft was a considerable departure from the water-cooled, in-line type of engines which had produced the sleek, stream-lined winners of the last three contests. As previous and current post-war RAF fighters were all powered by radial engines that were relatively light, there was a good reason for seeing what sort of performance the trophy competition might produce with the Crusader.

This Air Ministry order for seven machines was the largest ever given for a British Schneider Trophy entry and was only matched by Italy in the following year. Also, on 1 October, even before the January meeting to decide the date of the next competition, a High Speed Flight was formed, consisting of excep-tional military personnel, to test and compete with the new aircraft, rather than relying on company pilots, as had previously been the case.

The S5

At Supermarine, Mitchell continued to place his faith in the newer mono-plane approach and proceeded to strive for improvements on the S4 design. He was also content to use the reliable but powerful Napier Lion engine. Indeed, in the discussion that followed the 1925 Buchanan lecture to the Royal Aeronautical Society, he had remarked, 'At one time I thought that the "Lion" engine was at a disadvantage with the American engines, but I have changed my views rather, and certainly consider the "Lion" is capable of win-ning the Schneider Cup.'

He must also have noted that the Curtiss CR-3 engine had been much more closely cowled than his S4 had been, thus allowing a slimmer fuse-lage. Accordingly, Mitchell (and Folland for Glosters) had consulted with Napiers, and the new Lion was designed whereby the engine's frontal area was reduced by repositioning the magnetos and contouring the cam covers of the three cylinder engine banks to mate with the engine fairings fore and aft. Thus, Mitchell was able to reduce the cross section of his fuse-lage – so drastically, in fact, that the pilot's cockpit was an extremely tight fit. The pilots sat on the floor of the machine, their legs almost horizontal and their shoulders coming up to and pressing against the underside of the cockpit coaming. The result was the slimmest fuselage of all the current and subsequent contenders.

Flight Lieutenant H.M. Schofield, one of the pilots of the RAF High Speed Flight which had just been created, described their visit to Supermarine 'for a fitting':

> The method of reaching the seat was to squeeze in sideways and down as far as possible so that the shoulders were below the top fairing, then turn to face the front, and in my case it needed no ordinary effort to get my shoulders home. There were many sighs of relief from the watching design staff when the last man had been 'tried-in', for it had been a near thing and it did look as though it was not going to be enough at times.

As there was insufficient room for the fuel tank in the fuselage, the starboard float was used. This expedient also had the advantage of giving the aircraft more stability in the air by lowering its centre of gravity. It would also help towards counteracting the torque of the engine which, during take-off, might be expected to cause the opposing float to dig in and swing the aircraft off line before it gained sufficient airspeed to be effectively governed by the control surfaces. Mitchell also offset the fuel-loaded starboard float an extra 8in from the centre line as an additional response to this expected problem.

However, the most telling improvement, apart from the more powerful engine promised by Napiers, was the estimated increase of about 24mph by the proposed change from the Lamblin type underwing radiators of the S4 to

ABOVE: The Supermarine S5 awaiting cowlings for its Napier Lion engine. Note the hinged cockpit cover to facilitate entry. (Courtesy of Solent Sky Museum)

a system akin to that adopted by the Curtiss racers and, subsequently, by the Italian Macchi M39.

The new radiators were to be made out of copper sheets, 8½in wide, with their outer surfaces formed to the contours of the upper and lower wing surfaces. Thus the outer sheeting, exposed to the cooling airflow, offered minimal additional drag. Corrugations on the inner surface of these radiators formed channels for the coolant and this was taken along troughs behind the rear wing spar, through the radiators and along the leading edge of the wing, and then pumped to a header tank behind the engine block. Attention was even paid to the effect of different paints on the effectiveness of the radiators. The engine oil was also cooled via tubes which ran along the outsides of the fuselage and up to a header tank behind the cockpit. (Not long after flying tests began, it was found necessary to increase the capacity of the tubing.)

In terms of structure, the Supermarine contender continued the move away from its S4 predecessor. In line with the company's other developments at the time, the new machine was of mixed metal and wood construction, with the all-metal fuselage being a stressed-skin structure (which looked towards the Spitfire), while the flying surfaces were, like those of the S4, of wooden construction and ply-covered. It was designated 'S5' as it represented a complete redesign of the previous monoplane and also incorporated the new information gained from meticulous work at the National Physical Laboratory test facilities, which had been sponsored by the Air Ministry.

Mitchell had sent down three models for wind tunnel testing: one was a shoulder-wing design with wing roots cranked down and supported by streamlined struts from the floats; a second model had a low wing, similarly braced by struts; and the third configuration was an all-wire-braced proposal with a low wing position to give favourable bracing-wire angles.

Biard's problems with forward vision during landing and take-off in the S4 no doubt influenced Mitchell's considerations and, eventually, the flat, low wing position was chosen, particularly as it had been found that wires offered less resistance than struts. The wire bracing gave additional 'belt and braces' protection against a possible failure that a cantilever wing might experience, and a diagonal box spar was also fitted between the main spars to strengthen the wing torsionally against aileron loads.

The new wire bracing between the floats and from the floats to the bottom of the wing also allowed a wire 'cage' to be completed, as the wires from the upper fuselage to the top of the wings were fixed immediately above the float bracing attachment points. Mitchell was clearly guarding against any wing flexing which might have contributed to the S4 crash; and, whatever Mitchell's private thoughts were about the need to step back from the revolutionary concept of the cantilevered S4, the pragmatic reversion to wire bracing also brought a further reduction of the weight and drag which had been represented by the sturdy float struts of the S4.

The balancing out of advantages and disadvantages attendant upon the wish to reduce frontal area and weight against the need to ensure adequate strength and pilot view, was set out by Mitchell after the race in his speech to the Royal Aeronautical Society in 1927:

(a) The primary object in lowering the wing on the fuselage was to improve the view of the pilot, which was never very good on the S4. The higher position of the wing no doubt gave a lower resistance due to fairing in the outside engine blocks and thus saving a certain mount of frontal area. A loss in speed of about 3mph is estimated from this alteration. This loss is more than balanced, however, by the importance of the improved view.

(b) The system of wire bracing of the wings to the fuselage and floats was adopted for a number of reasons. The unbraced wings and chassis of the S4 were very high in structure weight, and it was found very difficult to construct an unbraced wing sufficiently strong and rigid without making it very thick at the root, and thus increasing its resistance. The adoption of bracing was largely responsible for a reduction in structure weight of 45 per cent for the S4 to 36 per cent for the S5, with its corresponding reduction in resistance; also for the elimination of the two struts between the floats, and for the reduction in frontal area of the four main chassis struts. Against these must be set the addition of fourteen wires. It is not easy to estimate the final effect of a number of alterations of this nature, but from the analysis of the resistance of the two machines it is given on fairly good grounds that the overall effect was an appreciable saving in resistance, amounting to an increase in speed of approximately 5mph.

(c) The cross-sectional area of the fuselage has been reduced by about 35 per cent. This very large reduction was obtained through the redesign of the engine and the very closely fitting fuselage. This almost amounted to a duralumin skin in order to ensure that the very smallest amount of cross-sectional area was added. On several occasions during the construction of the fuselage the pilots were fitted, and much trouble was experienced through their being of varying dimensions … The reduction in body resistance was responsible for an increase in speed of approximately 11mph.

The floats were also reduced in frontal area by about 14 per cent. This was accomplished by using a much lower reserve buoyancy. The reserve buoyancy was 55 per cent for the 'S4' floats and 40 per cent.

for the starboard float of the 'S5' [now being used for fuel tankage]. This figure is extremely low and called for very efficient lines.

The estimated increase in speed due to reduction in float resistance is 4mph. These reductions in resistance of fuselage and floats are due to lower cross-sectional areas and not to improvements in form.

(d) Wing-surface radiators were first fitted to the American machines in the 1925 race, and gave these machines a very big advantage in speed. The radiators added a certain amount of resistance to the machine due to their external corrugations increasing the area of exposed surface. As about 70 per cent. of the resistance of a high speed wing is skin friction, and the corrugations almost double the area of surface, it is reasonable to suppose that an increase of at least 30 per cent. of resistance is added to the wing. It is evident that a saving in resistance would result if radiators could be made with a flat outer surface, and that they would give no direct resistance to the machine. After much experimental work, radiators with a flat outer surface were produced. The chief difficulty experienced was in sufficiently strengthening and supporting the outer skin to enable it to stand the heavy air loads without making the radiators unduly heavy. The estimated increase of speed due to their use in place of Lamblin radiators used on the 'S4' is 24mph.

He could have also mentioned that, with the second S5 (which was to come first in the forthcoming contest), 'the hundreds of tiny rivets all over the skin were now flush with the surface instead of projecting like a mass of wee knobs as they had done'. This reminiscence of Schofield looks forward to a similar concern with the Spitfire (mentioned on p.180).

The result of all these design considerations culminated in a machine which, when it went to Venice to compete in the 1927 Schneider Trophy, was seen by the Italians as a direct copy of their Macchi M39, which had won the previous year. While Mitchell, like other engineers, was perfectly willing to profit from the successful design solutions of others (see pp.119–20, his Dornier-inspired Air Yacht), the Italian criticism had not taken into account Mitchell's trendsetting S4 of 1925, how long Mitchell had been contemplating his latest design, or how the wind tunnel tests had influenced his more pragmatic choice of this layout.

Nor did matters begin well for the British team as a whole. Bad weather prevented test flying until 10 September, only thirteen days before the required navigation tests were due. Then, on the following day, the Short Crusader crashed – it was found that the aileron controls had been crossed during re-rigging. The second batch of British planes arrived on 11 September, but bad weather again prevented test flying until the 21st, when it was found that the problem of fumes in the cockpits still needed attention. Both Supermarine and Gloster had discovered this problem before leaving for Venice but now one pilot, Flight Lieutenant S.M. Kinkead, was confined to his room all the next day. His machine also required attention as part of his spinner had come adrift, causing severe vibration.

The three permitted British entries were finalised as Flight Lieutenant S.N. Webster in the Supermarine N220, Flight Lieutenant O.E. Worsley in the Supermarine N219 and Kinkead in the better of the two Glosters. It was decided that the Supermarine N220 and the Gloster N223, with the unproven geared engines, were to fly flat-out in the expectation that Worsley, in the ungeared S5, would finish if, for any reason, the engines in the other two more complex machines failed.

Large crowds began to gather, and not just the locals who were strongly supporting the 'local boy', Captain Arturo Ferrarin. Major Mario de Bernardi was also a national favourite, having come first previously in the competition, and he was therefore well supported by those brought in by the Italian State Railway on special half-fare excursions. Unfortunately, a strong wind and a heavy swell made conditions too problematic for the sensitive floatplanes and the crowds had to return on 26 September, when conditions had improved. It was possible to commence the contest at 2.30 p.m. when Kinkead took off in the Gloster, followed by Webster and then de Bernardi. The new member of the Italian team, Captain Frederico Guazzetti, was next, then Worsley and, finally, Ferrarin.

Ferrarin soon disappointed his local supporters by turning off the course on the first lap with two pistons burnt through, followed by de Bernardi on lap two, suffering from a connecting rod failure. The third Macchi, with an older replacement engine, proved no match for the British with their new uprated Lions, but then Kinkead retired at the beginning of the sixth lap when violent vibrations made it seem prudent to do so. This turned out to have been a wise decision as the previous vibrations were now found to have caused a shear-line about three-quarters around the circumference of the propeller shaft. Then, on the penultimate lap and in sight of being placed, the last Italian, Guazzetti, pulled out in spectacular fashion when he was blinded by the bursting of a petrol pipe. Luckily, he managed to get down safely, although not before just missing spectators on the roof of the Excelsior Hotel on the Lido.

Webster (watched by Mussolini) led the British whitewash with an average speed of 281.65mph, a new record for seaplanes and bettering by 3mph the world speed record for land planes. Worsley came second at 273.01mph in the second, ungeared, S5.

The skill of the pilots is demonstrated by the fact that the RAF front-line fighter at this time, the Armstrong Whitworth Siskin IIIA, had a top speed of only 186mph and that, despite light rain and haze towards the end of the competition, both men, while having to negotiate two sharp turns per lap, had averaged about 87 per cent of the maximum speed available to them. As Schofield said, 'It must be remembered that we were the first service team, that our work … carried with it an increase in speed of a proportion unheard of before'. It ought also to be added that this unprecedented leap in speeds took place in racing aircraft with the low cockpit positions mentioned earlier, which gave extremely limited, almost non-existent forward views.

When Mitchell, with his wife, arrived back in England, he was among those feted by the Corporation of Southampton and his winning machine was put on display in London. A measure of the designer's increased status can also be gained by his being invited to address the Royal Aeronautical Society at this time.

In 1928, Vickers (Aviation) Limited acquired the Supermarine Company, but acknowledged the achievements of Mitchell's design team by retaining it as an entity at Woolston and by allowing the branch a separate identity. Thus, in subsequent volumes of *Jane's*, publication of designs from Mitchell's team were kept separate from other Vickers products under the following title: The Supermarine Aviation Works Ltd (Division of Vickers (Aviation) Ltd).

Vickers had no doubt acknowledged the potential of the much smaller company as early as 1920 when its Commercial Amphibian came a very close second to their Viking. Then came the orders for the Sea Eagle, the Seagull, the Scarab and, pre-eminently, the Southampton. However, in view of Vickers' dominant position in the armaments industry, Mitchell's high speed Schneider Trophy contributions must have been particularly noted and thus made Supermarine's unexpected design of the Spitfire that much more probable.

Mitchell's name now appeared among the list of Vickers directors, and the 1925 publicity description of him as 'one of the leading flying boat and amphibian designers in the country' was now significantly expanded to: 'one of the leading flying boat, amphibian and high speed seaplane designers in the country'.

He was 34 years old.

THE FLYING RADIATORS

After Britain's Schneider Trophy success in Venice, the world speed record was raised by the rival Italian Macchi M52, now that its engine problems had been overcome.

Flight Lieutenant Kinkead, who had now taken command of the High Speed Flight, attempted a challenge in the third S5, which had been held in reserve in Italy, but he was killed when he appeared to fly into the sea at full speed, perhaps because of some structural failure – contrary to the official inquest finding that the pilot stalled when attempting to land, because of poor visibility.

Flight Lieutenant D'Arcy Greig took over the flight, and the trophy-winning Supermarine S5 was now prepared for a further attempt. However, the speed achieved did not give a margin sufficient to justify a claim to the FAI and it was clear that a substantial improvement upon the British aircraft would be necessary in time for the defence of the trophy, especially as it would take place in front of a home crowd.

In 1927, Britain and Mitchell had been more fortunate than the Italians as their winning engine had not been a new, and therefore possibly unreliable, design. However, the Napier Lion had been in continuous development since its use in the Supermarine 1922 Schneider Trophy winner and, although it had never failed in the aircraft it powered, the question had nevertheless to be asked whether this remarkable engine was now reaching the end of its development potential.

By now, Rolls-Royce had produced the successful 490hp Kestrel, in response to the American Curtiss D-1 engine which had powered the Schneider Trophy-winning aircraft of 1923 and 1925. The Kestrel now offered reduction gearing and supercharging and Mitchell asked Major G.P. Bulman, the Air Ministry official responsible for the development of aero engines, for his opinions. Bulman thought that Rolls-Royce should be approached, and Mitchell was reported to have given it some thought and then said, 'Right, that's decided it.'

Commander James Bird, the managing director of Supermarine, and Bulman accordingly called on Henry Royce, then living in semi-retirement at his West Wittering home on the Sussex coast and, as it was already October 1928, it was decided that the partially developed 36.7-litre Buzzard engine would have to be the basis for the required new engine. It would have to have a modified crankcase and supercharger to conform to the sort of shape that Mitchell was likely to develop out of the S5 design and so it was separately designated the 'R' engine, with a hoped for output of 1,800hp.

The S6

For the improved airframe, Mitchell decided on the basic suitability of his previous design for the more powerful new engine. Thus his main design effort was in respect of a larger, all-metal, version of the S5, in order to accommodate the projected heavier engine: the 930lb of the Napier Lion in 1927 was to be replaced by an engine weighing 1530lb.

First configuration drawings were sent to Mitchell on 3 July 1928, and he was able to influence the shape of the cam covers so that they would conform to the streamlines he was developing for his new machine. An eventual 1900hp was achieved by August – a power increase of 211 per cent over the previous Lion engine, for what turned out to be a loaded aircraft weight increase of 78 per cent.

Mitchell was reported to have said, 'Go steady with your horsepower' – no doubt anticipating the cooling problems that would be encountered.

An immediately obvious alteration to the new machine was the cowling, necessitated by the change from the 'arrow' shape of the Lion engine to the 'V' of the new Rolls-Royce unit. As the empty weight of the S6 was 1791lb heavier than that of the S5, the wingspan was increased by more than 3ft and the front float struts had to be moved further forward on the fuselage to support the heavier and longer engine. Also, the increase in fuel consumption, from the Lion engine with a 24-litre capacity to the proposed Rolls-Royce R engine of 36.7 litres, would require both floats to be used for the fuel tanks and the extra weight of the new engine made it necessary to move the pilot's position further back.

Solving the constructional and loading problems in itself had justified the new design's 'S6' designation, but these matters were relatively straightforward compared to contending with the heat produced by the new engine.

The channels for oil cooling attached to the sides of the fuselage of the S5 were now increased, more were added to the underside of the fuselage, and particular attention was given to their efficiency. Mitchell's chief metallurgist, Arthur Black, came up with a solution whereby the channels which conveyed the oil from and to the engine had copper tongues soldered at right angles to the oil flow, and these were configured in such a way that they did not impede the flow of oil, while ensuring its maximum contact with the surfaces of the piping being cooled by the slipstream of the aircraft.

Additionally, the oil was now sprayed from this piping into the top of the fin to trickle down to the return pipes, thereby causing the fin to act as both oil tank and radiator. It was estimated that these devices increased the efficiency of the oil cooling by about 40 per cent but, nevertheless, Greig found that the position of the oil piping, attached to the sides and base of a very narrow fuselage, 'turned the inside of the cockpit into something approaching an extremely hot Turkish bath' with the oil temperature gauge reading 'around 136 degrees centigrade'.

Other aspects of the design reflected the constructional changes beginning to take place in the aircraft industry, and Supermarine were anxious to point out that their move to metal construction was not just with respect to the framework of their machine, but placed them in the forefront of the use of load-bearing external skinning – particularly in respect of the wings. Here, instead of being plywood covered with the radiator panels externally attached, as with the S5, they were now covered by the panels alone. Now made of aluminium, the radiator panels now took torsional loads and, as Supermarine announced, 'saved a considerable amount of weight over previous practice'.

Despite the gap of two years between competitions that had now been agreed upon, the scheduled start of the eleventh event was less than six weeks away before Mitchell's new airframes could be tested in the air. In May, the new R engine had reached 1545hp but, after running for about quarter of an hour, failures began to occur and it was only at the end of July that the new engine passed the one hour mark at full throttle and supercharger boost. A few days later, with the blending of a special fuel, an engine run of 100 minutes and 1850hp was achieved.

Incidentally, the end of testing was much to the relief of the citizens of Derby, as the tests had also required the running of three Kestrel aero engines. They drove fans to cool the new R engine, to expel fumes from the test shed, and to enable the carburettors to be set up in simulated flight conditions. These were the days before modern health and safety regulations, and Rodwell Banks, responsible for the fuel mixes, described the din of four aero engines within the test sheds: 'reverberation from walls and roof is such that at certain engine speeds one cannot keep still: the whole body seems in a state of high frequency vibration. One shouts at the top of one's voice but cannot even feel the vibration of the vocal chords.'

People living up to 15 miles away reported still being able to hear the engine runs, and the ears of the Rolls-Royce workers were plugged with cotton wool. They were also well supplied with milk to counteract the laxative effect of breathing in the engine oil, ejected out of the exhaust ports and deposited on the walls of the test cell. *Flight* reported that one early run consumed oil at the rate of 112 gallons per hour and that the state of the test shed inside was 'a wonder to behold'.

Meanwhile, a new High Speed Flight had been formed in the February of 1928. Greig, who had been posted in after the death of Kinkead, had recommended members of his Hendon aerobatic team: Flight Lieutenants G.H. Stainforth and R.D.H. Waghorn and Flying Officer R.L.R. Atcherley. He then prepared to hand over command to a Squadron Leader, A.H. Orlebar, with the new title, 'Officer Commanding the High Speed Flight'. As before, none of these airmen had been trained as naval pilots, and so time was needed to convert onto the seaplanes that were expected to be the fastest in the world.

Waghorn has described how they used their practice machines to devise the best method for cornering with the help of scientists from the Royal Aircraft Establishment, who installed instruments in the machines to measure speed, acceleration and climb. A compromise between high G tight turns, with loss of speed, and wider arcs, which incurred less drag, was worked out. But, with the increased speed in the turns, pilots had now to get used to blacking out, as Atcherley recalled:

I went 'out' halfway round a turn at Calshot Castle [the sharpest of the four turns of the proposed course] and flew completely unconscious at about 500ft halfway back to Cowes before regaining my senses. Even then, there was a very frightening lapse of seconds when one realised that one *was* flying and had been 'out' but still could not see or move one's hands.

As the circuit flying took place at an altitude of only a few hundred feet, he unsurprisingly admitted that 'it made me brood a bit'.

These preparations received a considerable setback when the actual contest aircraft finally arrived and it was discovered that the possible effects of the much greater torque of the new engine had not been fully appreciated. Against the turn of the propeller, the S6 would dig in the left float, describing circles in the water which Orlebar reported 'had rather shaken' Mitchell. One can easily imagine the chief designer's feelings, seeing his aircraft quite unwilling to fly, and when Orlebar pointed out to him that 247, the number of the first of the new machines, added up to thirteen, 'the poor chap replied with feeling that he had not designed that'.

A solution to the torque problem at take-off would be found in later years with the invention of variable pitch propellers but, in the meantime, a special technique was worked out whereby it was necessary to keep the stick well back, contrary to all basic instruction, in order to maximise lift at the extreme low end of the aircraft's airspeed. Additionally, the take-off had to begin with any breeze kept on the left quarter. This allowed for a nice judgement of acceleration while being pulled in an arc by the propeller torque to face directly into wind by the time that lift-off speed was attained.

To assist the pilots, Mitchell lengthened the starboard float by 1ft so that it could contain 90 gallons of fuel and allow the capacity of the submerging float to be reduced to 25 gallons. But having now achieved take-off, engine overheating was found to be a problem and so radiator piping had to be fitted along the sides of the floats. Small scoops were also fitted under the wing tips, facing forward and, with exhaust ports at the wing roots, creating a flow of air over the inner surfaces of the radiators – an unexpected bonus for using the radiators as load-bearing wing surfaces.

Once these problems had been overcome, and if one set aside the peculiarities of the take-off procedures, the S6s were proving to be viceless aircraft to fly and to have even better flying qualities than the previous, smaller, less powerful machine, despite the wing loading having now risen from 28 to 40lb/sq. ft. Waghorn wrote that, although she was a little heavier laterally, there was no noticeable torque effect against a left-hand turn which he had found tiring in the S5. He also found the new machine 'extraordinarily stable at the stall', whereas the S5 would quiver and 'flick over either side at the slightest provocation'. The S6 showed no tendency to drop either wing, but would sink on an even keel – no doubt much appreciated by the pilots, as the 'ground effect' of the low wing and the highly streamlined fuselage created a long 'float' at over 100mph before final touch down.

Meanwhile, the two Gloster VIs were affected by 'G' related fuel starvation problems, and the Italians, the only other team to compete in 1929, were experiencing worse problems. They had also received their new aircraft late, and it was soon found that the hydrofoil equipped Piaggio P.7 was unable to take off at all, and one of the two Fiat C29s caught fire and later stalled on take-off and sank.

On the other hand, the first of the Macchi M67s was looking much more promising, reaching a speed of over 360mph, but then it too crashed, killing its pilot. Accordingly, Italy requested a one-month postponement on 22 August, but the Royal Aero Club stuck to the rules and refused the next day – the FAI concurred.

To prevent Britain winning by a fly-over, Italy decided not to withdraw from the competition and sent over their remaining, largely untested, aircraft – the second Fiat C29, a Savoia-Marchetti S65 and the two Macchi M67s – as well as two older Macchi M52s, one of which currently held the world speed record. By this time, both the Supermarine aircraft were ready but, as the Glosters' fuel problems could not be solved in time, it was decided to call up one of the 1927 S5s.

Perhaps surprisingly, all the aircraft successfully completed the competition navigation tests on 6 September and they were then all moored out for the watertightness test. Some time later, Mitchell, having been up late overseeing final preparations, was woken up in the officers' mess. Atcherley's N248 was listing, still with over two hours to go of the required flotation test. Mitchell decided that it would hold out long enough and went back to bed. By the due time, the machine had a very distinct list but was able to be beached and a leak repaired.

Then a further, more serious, problem was discovered, this time with Waghorn's N247. Traces of white metal were found during the routine plug change and internal damage strongly suspected. The competition rules did not allow 'any major component' to be changed at this late stage, but it was at least possible to substitute parts. Orlebar has recounted that 'poor Mitchell was hauled out again' as the required removal and replacement of one of the cylinder blocks was going to present a problem.

Major overhauls would normally be carried out at Rolls-Royce with the engine removed from the aircraft but, at Calshot, it was necessary to devise some means of offering the intact machine up to the replacement block. Luckily, a number of Rolls-Royce mechanics had travelled to see the competition and they were collected from various hotels nearby. By working through the early hours of the morning, they were able to make the change, even without manoeuvring the aircraft. Their heroic efforts were proved entirely necessary, as it was found that one piston head and its cylinder lining was damaged and would have led, at the very least, to engine failure in the competition. The damage was traced to fuel being drawn into the engine during slow running before take-off and washing lubricant from the cylinder walls. It was thereafter decided that no engine was to have long periods of slow running prior to the beginning of the contest.

British tactics had also to take account of the fact that the cooling of the S6s was so critical that a water temperature of 95° had not to be exceeded. So it was decided that Waghorn would fly as fast as possible, consistent with keeping to a safe engine temperature; that Atcherley, in the second S6, would risk a higher temperature if the performances of the two preceding Italians made it necessary to go faster than Waghorn; and that Greig, in the slower S5, would provide additional back-up.

In the event, Waghorn began with a slower than expected first lap owing to a rather wayward flight path, as vessels on the course had made it hard for him to identify the ship-borne pylon marking the second turn. Then the Italian in the first M67 retired on lap two as he had been nearly blinded and suffocated by fumes from his exhaust.

Atcherley also had a visibility problem caused by spray from a long take-off run; he tried to replace his goggles with a substitute pair but these were swept away in his slipstream. He carried on, but nearly killed himself when at the very last moment he saw the first pylon and had to swerve sharply to avoid it. As his evasive action had taken him inside the pylon, he was disqualified. Meanwhile, the pilot of the second M67 was also experiencing fume problems and was then forced to make a hasty landing when steam and nearly boiling water began blowing back from the engine.

In the end, Waghorn took first place with an average speed of 328.63mph, Dal Molin in the M52 was second with an average speed of 284.2mph and Greig came a close third with an average speed of 282.11mph. Atcherley was compensated for not being placed in the competition by achieving the World's Closed Circuit Speed Records for 50km and 100km at 332.49 and 331.75mph. respectively, on his sixth and seventh laps.

Press coverage and eulogy was sustained by an ensuing competition to establish a new World Absolute Air Speed Record between the S6 and the Gloster VI, whose fuel supply problems had now been overcome. The latter achieved 336.3mph three days after the Schneider contest, but Orlebar, as the CO of the High Speed Flight, fittingly took the record with 355.8mph. The existing Italian record of 318.62 was further exceeded two days later, on 12 September, when the S6 reached 357.7mph.

Waghorn's winning S6.

With the possibility of a third win in 1931, and therefore the outright capture of the Schneider Trophy, Supermarine and Rolls-Royce began discussions with the Air Ministry in respect of a predicted increase of 25mph on the Schneider course, assuming that the S6 machines would be loaned back for uprating and that they would be piloted by High Speed Flight pilots. The cost of a successful defence of the trophy was estimated to be in the region of £100,000 and involved the production of two improved machines and engines to support them but, in view of the worsening economic climate, the government now declined any help whatsoever.

The response, especially in aviation circles, was outrage – but to no avail. Fortunately, the formidable and extremely wealthy Lady Houston was approached and she promised what was then the enormous sum of £100,000 to sponsor Britain's entry and, incidentally, to embarrass the Labour Prime Minister and his government. By the time some political points had been scored and the necessary money allocated, there was less than a year left for all the work required in time for the competition in the coming September.

Because of this time constraint and the finite funds available, the British hopes would be concentrated upon uprating the current Rolls-Royce engine and upon modifying the existing S6 design to handle an expected increase in power. Derby had, once more, to put up with the noise of the engine testing and its mayor had to appeal to the patriotism of its citizens. The tests ran from 1 April–12 August before the uprated engine could run for an hour at full power – by which time the 1900hp of the 1929 engine had been increased to 2350hp.

The S6B

In view of this power increase, Supermarine estimated that the new aircraft would have to dissipate 'something like 40,000 BT units' every minute – the equivalent of over 300 modern fan heaters operating at full power. Mitchell had, therefore, to provide additional radiator surfaces on the floats right down to their chines so that almost half of the 948sq. ft of the aircraft's available surface area was now to be used for cooling. It is understandable why Mitchell, in a radio broadcast after the competition, described his new aircraft as a 'flying radiator'.

Enlarging the cooling area was assisted by an increase in the size of the floats, as the anticipated fuel consumption of the new engine required their capacity to be enlarged, as did a modification to the competition rules – the aircraft were now required to take-off and land immediately prior to the start of the race proper, instead of the navigability and seaworthiness tests being carried out with minimal fuel the day before.

Wind tunnel testing at the National Physical Laboratory and tank testing at Vickers, nevertheless, led to a narrower float design, although of increased length. The side plating was extended knifelike by ¾in below the chines and as far as the step, to improve running and to inhibit spray. The elevators no longer had a 'v' cut-out close to the fuselage but were now made to operate with minimum clearance in order to reduce turbulence at this point.

The revised design was accordingly designated S6B and it was possible to afford two, with the serials S1595 and S1596. Additionally the two 1929 machines, N247 and N248, were uprated and, as such, they were redesignated S6A. The only noticeable difference between the two pairs of machines was that the latter had its original floats, which were 2ft shorter than those of 1931.

As there were now four Supermarine racers available, Flying Officer L.S. Snaith was added to the High Speed Flight, already consisting of Flight Lieutenants J.N. Bootham, E.J.L. Hope, F.W. Long and G.H. Stainforth. Flying with the contest machines began when N247 arrived on 20 May, but an alarming oscillation of the rudder developed during an early high speed run, causing the buckling of rear fuselage plates, stress cracks around some of the rivet holes and stretched control wires. In the short time available, Mitchell had streamlined weights on forward projecting brackets fitted to both sides of the rudder and the ailerons – in order to bring the centre of gravity of these surfaces to coincide with their hinge lines and so to dampen any future oscillations which might occur. The last bay of the fuselage was also strengthened.

Weights were also needed in response to some instability on take-off and during turns. Mitchell decided that the problem here was due to the centre of gravity being too far back and so he had about 25lb of lead placed in the nose of each float and reduced the amount of oil (which was, again, carried all the way back to a tank in the fin). However, Orlebar had also reported nose-heaviness during level flight, and Mitchell (before the developing use of trim tabs) 'produced a splendid gadget to cure the trouble' – metal strips were fitted to the trailing edge of the elevators and bent downwards by about one degree, thus using the slipstream at high speed to deflect the elevator upwards slightly and to counteract any load on the stick.

Additionally, the engines were prone to cutting out because of choked fuel filters. This was found to be the result of the engine's exotic fuel mixture causing the excess compound used to seal the joints in the fuel system to come adrift. Mitchell's response was both practical and blunt: 'You'll just have to bloody well fly them until all this stuff comes out.'

There was another problem previously experienced in 1927 – the first new S6B, which had arrived on 21 July, could not be made to fly as it also gyrated in 'a very good imitation of a kitten chasing its tail'. In the course of these rotations, S1595 hit a barge and had to be returned from Calshot for repair. As a new reason for its unwillingness to take off was suspected, the smaller 8ft 8in diameter propeller of the S6B was fitted to N247, which then behaved like its younger sister. This suggested that the slipstream from this diameter propeller was producing a side pressure that the rudder was unable to counteract. When S1595 was returned on 29 July, a larger diameter unit was fitted and the new machine then took off with little difficulty.

In view of the peculiar take-off requirements mentioned earlier, the increased speed, and the extra weight of the new aircraft, it is not surprising that the British team now began to have accidents. Mitchell had to watch the pilots of his machines flying at previously unattained speeds, virtually at sea level, often in hazy conditions, and taking off and landing without the aid of flaps or variable pitch propellers, among the busy shipping lanes off Calshot.

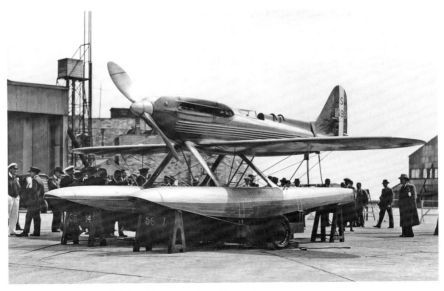

The first of the S6Bs at Calshot. (Courtesy of E.B. Morgan)

Hope virtually wrote off one of the S6A machines. A piece of the cowling from N248 worked loose in flight and, while managing an emergency landing, he encountered the wash from a passing ship, which caused the sensitive machine to cartwheel and sink. The pilot survived, but was withdrawn from the team because of a punctured eardrum. (He was the son of the influential hull designer mentioned in Chapter 2; as Group Captain Linton Hope, AFC, he was killed in action in August 1941.)

Hope was replaced by Lieutenant G.L. Brinton who, on 18 August and on his first take-off in N247, was killed. D'Arcy Greig had explained how, if porpoising developed during take-off and with the stick held well back, it was imperative to close the throttle and start again; otherwise, the pitching of the aircraft invariably increased until the machine was eventually thrown into the air in a stalled condition and an accident was inevitable. Like the pilot of the Sea Lion III before him, Brinton apparently did not fully appreciate the importance of this advice, and *Time* magazine reported that:

The plane slid along the surface of the Solent until it was going about 200mph. It cleared the water for a second and then dropped back to it. A tower of spray shot up. The S6 bounced 40ft in the air and then plunged down into the Solent, nose first. When Lieut. Brinton's fellow officers reached the ship in a speedboat, it had risen again, upside down, with wings and tail torn off. The wreckage was towed ashore and the dead body of Lieut. Brinton removed from the tail of the fuselage, where the shock had wedged it.

Flight Lieutenant Long on his return from a test run. (Courtesy of P. Jarrett)

The writer did not elaborate on the fate of Brinton's body. It was first assumed to have been lost at sea and only later was it found jammed into the rear of the fuselage. It is not recorded how news of the actual discovery of the body was received by Mitchell but, in view of his well-known concern for the pilots of his machines, an explanation of the need to cut into the damaged machine for its recovery must have required considerable tact.

At about the same time, a French aircraft was considerably damaged in a landing accident and another was completely destroyed, killing its pilot. Meanwhile, Macchi were developing their M67 layout into a new machine, which was also to kill one of its pilots. The main feature of the new aircraft was the advanced engineering of contra-rotating propellers, but the revolutionary power plant was plagued with problems, especially carburation, and during a fly-past to demonstrate its erratic behaviour, it crashed, also killing its pilot.

As a result of such accidents and other setbacks, the French and Italian teams jointly requested a postponement of at least six months. As some government assistance in the matter of RAF support had eventually been won with difficulty, as funds had already been spent in preparations for a competition that was virtually only days away and as Lady Houston's generous donation had been used up, the due date of the event was insisted on. As a result, the Air Ministry was informed on 5 September that neither France nor Italy felt able to compete.

In the end, the only postponement of what was expected to be a fly-over for Britain was for one day owing to bad weather, and the following day was almost perfect with visibility of over 10 miles. In view of there being no external competition, it was decided that S1595 was to fly the course without putting undue strain on the engine – the increase in propeller diameter had resulted in too high an engine temperature and, again, Mitchell had had to accept a slightly lower airspeed than his design was capable of. If S1595 were to fail, then Hope's repaired S6A would be sent off to finish the course and, therefore, to win the trophy outright. The second S6B would also be available to make trebly sure of a win, but it was hoped to retain this aircraft to give the crowds the additional thrill of seeing the setting of a new world speed record.

The commanding officer, Orlebar, gave his senior pilot, Stainforth, first choice and he opted for the proposed attempt on the speed record. The next most senior man, Boothman, then chose to fly first in the competition itself and, it was hoped, to have the honour of winning the trophy. And so, just before 1 p.m. on 13 September, Boothman taxied out in S1595, which he had never flown in practice for longer than twenty-seven minutes. Nor had it been considered wise to practice the landing, as the 1931 rules required, with the full load of fuel for both the 350km of the competition course and for the required preliminary navigation manoeuvres.

Nevertheless, he took off without any apparent difficulty, made the required landing at well over 100mph without mishap, and took off again after a period of less than two minutes. He then flew the required seven laps, all within about 4mph of each other, slightly throttled back, taking the turns wide and with a gentle bank and finished with an average speed of 340.08mph – just over 11mph faster than Waghorn in 1929. Then, as if to emphasise the superiority of the Rolls-Royce/Supermarine partnership and also to post a more impressive speed, Stainforth took out the other S6B a little later and proceeded to capture the World Absolute Air Speed Record at 379.05mph.

Lady Houston had attended on her steam yacht to watch 'her' machines and, two days later, gave a celebratory lunch on board, attended by Mitchell and his wife and by the High Speed Flight. Cozens recorded that:

> She was afforded the rare privilege of mooring her yacht *Liberty* on the RAF buoys inside Calshot … In the evenings the *Liberty* had a string of electric lights from her bowsprit to the mastheads and down to the stern, and this seemed to add just the right touch to the celebration of victory.

The Air Ministry then set about disbanding the High Speed Flight and restoring the Calshot base to its normal flying boat duties, but Rolls-Royce particularly wanted to have produced the first aero engine to exceed the magic mark of 400mph. Mitchell had indicated the same in an interview with the Southampton *Daily Echo*, when he said that 'with a specially tuned up engine, I am very hopeful we may get very near to an average speed of 400mph, which is our ambition'.

For this special sprint machine, Mitchell had the wing-tip air scoops removed and a newly prepared engine was to be supplied, using a specially blended fuel mixture. After delays caused by the weather, Stainforth squeezed into the cockpit of S1595 and the required runs were photographically measured. There was some concern that bad light and a low evening sun might prevent confirmation being obtained, but eventually, at 4 a.m., the results were telephoned through and Mitchell was informed. It was reported that he was 'too sleepy to be more than mildly enthusiastic' that the World Absolute Speed Record had just been raised by nearly 30mph to 407.5mph.

An invitation to give a talk on the BBC in 1932 indicated recognition by the wider public of his technical achievements, and his name appeared in the New Year's Honours List of that year. Mitchell particularly disliked having to wear bows on his Court shoes but it was surely impossible for one who had designed so many aircraft for the British armed forces not to accept becoming a Commander of the Order of the British Empire.

As Mitchell always gave full credit to others in his speeches, there is no reason to suppose that he would begrudge, in this chapter concerning his notable Schneider Trophy successes, a final word about the pilots concerned. Various instances of their skill and courage are to be found in the preceding pages, including flying and alighting at unprecedented speeds, in machines with extremely limited vision, and at altitudes that gave little margins for error and no possibility of survival if things went badly wrong.

Mitchell greeting Lady Houston at Calshot on the occasion of the 1931 Schneider Trophy Contest. (Courtesy of Solent Sky Museum)

Undoubtedly, other pilots would have accepted the challenges of flying beyond the boundaries of previous experience, but it was those mentioned above to whom credit must go. If they had not successfully flown their frankly dangerous aircraft, the Spitfire might not have been ready in time for the Battle of Britain. One notes, at least, D'Arcy Greig's dedication in *My Golden Flying Years* 'to all those involved with the Schneider Trophy races that helped so much in the development of the Spitfire in later years'.

6

THE LAST SEAPLANES

MITCHELL'S AIR YACHTS

R.J. Mitchell was responsible for two luxury air yachts, although both in fact began as military orders. The first looked backwards to the Southampton reconnaissance flying boat, but the second might very well have led to a Supermarine equivalent of the Catalina, which became the most widely used maritime patrol aircraft in the Second World War.

The Solent

The first Air Yacht came about as a request from Denmark for a torpedo-carrying version of the Southampton; it was to be called 'Nanok', the Inuit word for polar bear, and first flew in 1927. But all was not well, as the necessary positioning of the torpedoes produced stability problems. As each torpedo was suspended fairly well out from the centre line of the flying boat, the resultant lurches when dropping only one torpedo, necessarily at low level, could hardly have recommended the aircraft to any pilot assessing it.

The three-engined layout that had been requested by Denmark was also found to produce trim problems, because the additional power at the high thrust line caused the machine to become distinctly nose heavy as power increased. Mitchell's response was to fit a somewhat ad hoc auxiliary stabiliser higher up between the three fins, but this lowered the flying speed below that contracted for. And so, in the end, the Royal Danish Navy took delivery of a standard Southampton instead.

Fortunately, in 1928, the Honourable A.E. Guinness was persuaded of the potential of a private flying boat, in addition to *Fantome*, the largest and most spectacular barque-rigged yacht in the British registry. Thus the unwanted

ABOVE: The Supermarine Solent. (Courtesy of E.B. Morgan)

PREVIOUS: Supermarine Walruses. (From a painting by the author)

Nanok was converted into an 'Air Yacht' with comfortable cabins for up to twelve passengers. Now named 'Solent' and registered G-AAAB, it soon became a familiar sight, flying from the Hythe seaplane base on Southampton Water to Lough Corrib, County Galway, close to Ashford Castle, its owner's home.

The Air Yacht

The second Air Yacht was to follow in 1930 and began as an Air Ministry specification, calling for an armed reconnaissance flying boat. At this time, one might have expected a traditional metal-hulled biplane but, instead, what eventually appeared was an uncompromising all-metal monoplane with a wingspan of 92ft and powered by three engines which were now faired into the wings – as with all Mitchell's later multi-engined flying boats.

It had a plank-shaped parasol wing with sloping V struts supporting the wing about two-thirds out from the centre line. The hull, instead of the curvaceous design made famous with the Southampton, was a slab-sided type, strengthened with horizontal corrugations; it also had extremely angular fins in keeping with the rest of the general arrangement. The new design still had fabric-covered flying surfaces but it had one feature which made it stand out from all other Supermarine aircraft and its contemporaries, and this was the employment of sponsons attached to the lower sides of the hull instead of the customary wing-tip floats.

However, despite its unique appearance among British aircraft, its similarity to the (smaller) German Dornier Wal series of flying boats was, to say the least, very close (see drawing overleaf). In fact, one of the Wal machines had been tested at Calshot, and Denis le P. Webb, who had joined Supermarine in 1926, later wrote: 'my impression was that R.J., who had always been more of a

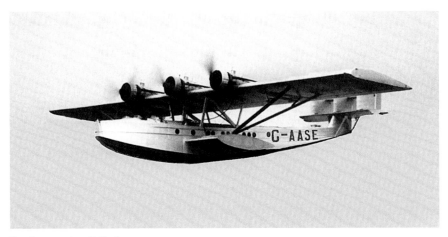

The Supermarine Air Yacht.

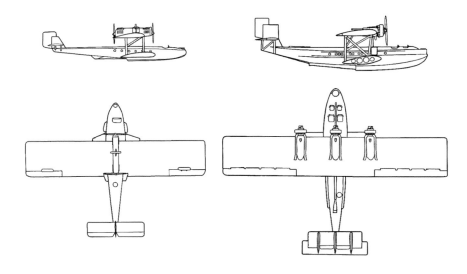

Dornier Wal.   Air Yacht.

practical engineer than technician, had allowed himself to be lured by some of
his bright boys into following other people's ideas instead of his own.'

Perhaps because it was such a departure from the well-tried Supermarine
biplane types, the new approach was not an immediate success. Its maximum speed was well below the 120mph that the joint Vickers/Supermarine
Southampton X achieved the following month, with only slightly more powerful engines. It was accordingly re-engined with 525hp Armstrong-Siddeley
Panthers and was then found to be capable of 117mph. However, it was still not
possible to maintain height with any significant payload when one of the three
engines was throttled back.

Despite the fact that the Short Singapore II biplane, built in the same year,
could achieve 140mph, the Air Ministry continued to support the novel
Supermarine monoplane by, at least, paying for repairs and for the replacement of the sponsons when they failed in fairly rough seas – giving the lie to
the usually held view that officialdom at that time was entirely hostile to the
monoplane concept.

Harald Penrose, reporting on the interwar aviation scene, did compare its
design favourably with two more traditionally-built flying boats, but recorded
that 'unfortunately the sponsons suffered battering by waves and even on calm
water gave inferior take-off compared with the usual chined British hull'.
Nevertheless, he went on to say that 'assessed as an engineering structure of
considerable aerodynamic cleanness, the Air Yacht was a big step forward compared with the established three-engined Iris biplane, of which four were in

the course of delivering to the RAF, or the Calcutta-derived Short Rangoon prototype due to fly in the summer'. (Or, in fact, compared with Mitchell's own subsequent biplanes, the Scapa and the Stranraer flying boats!)

Indeed, Penrose's suggestion that the Air Yacht might represent the future is supported by a comparison with the American Consolidated Commodore, which also had a parasol fabric-covered wing of about the same span. It appeared in the same year as Mitchell's machine but was far less clean, aerodynamically, with well over thirty supporting struts. But despite its potential promise, Harry Griffiths, another Supermarine employee, gave the Air Yacht a negative report:

> It had a very long take-off run and there was always doubt as to whether it would leave the water at all with a full load of passengers, stores and fuel. Refuelling in those days was done with hand pumps from barrels taken out on a barge. There is a story (unconfirmed but, knowing the man, possibly true) that Biard, the test pilot, refused to attempt a full load take-off and 'went through the motions' of filling with fuel by pumping from a number of barrels, some of which were empty.

And so, by 1931, Supermarine began to try to salvage matters by seeking civil registration (G-AASE), in the expectation of fulfilling an order from the Honourable A.E. Guinness for a replacement of his Solent Air Yacht.

The new machine's boxy hull certainly provided very advantageous dimensions for the passenger cabin, which Supermarine quoted as a generous 35ft length, 6ft 6in height and 8ft width. It was luxuriously appointed, with owner's cabin complete with bed, bath and toilet, a galley with full cooking facilities, and additional wash basins, toilet and comfortable lounge with settees and sideboards in a separate cabin for five other passengers. Electric lighting was fitted throughout the interior, which Biard described as 'one of the most luxurious that anyone had then seen' and 'fitted out in glass and silver, with deep-pile rugs underfoot ... the chairs were deeply sprung, the cabins softly lighted ... no offending smell of petrol or oil ever filtered into the passenger accommodation', and the temperature could even be regulated by a blown air system.

Unfortunately, Guinness turned to a Saunders-Roe product and the Air Yacht was put in storage until rescue came in the form of the formidable American, Mrs June Jewell James, a keen motorboat and flying enthusiast. Mrs James had been shown over the aircraft stored at the company's Hythe base and, as a result, she negotiated its purchase from Supermarine in 1932. She named her new acquisition 'Windward III' and became so impatient to have the use of her new purchase for a cruise to the Mediterranean and North Africa that she insisted on starting some days before the prearranged departure date.

Biard, who had been seconded to her by Supermarine, supplied a description of the frantic preparations and of the one, and only, cruise attempted in the aircraft. Despite some exaggerations, his (ghosted?) account is of interest to social historians as well as to those interested in the ability of another Mitchell design to withstand what were, clearly, extremely unfriendly conditions when it anchored in Cherbourg Harbour. After Mrs James and her companions were nearly drowned there in a fierce storm, Biard flew the Air Yacht down to Naples where Mrs James proceeded to obtain audiences with both the Pope and Mussolini.

Having flown to France to collect Mrs James, who had by now gone on to Paris, Biard had to hand over the Air Yacht at Naples to a relief pilot as his stomach muscles, which had been torn in the S4 crash of 1925, needed surgery. This pilot, Flight Lieutenant Thomas Rose, although very experienced, suffered an engine failure and stalled into the sea in the vicinity of Capri on 25 January. The owner suffered a broken leg, but otherwise there were no very serious injuries sustained; however, the aircraft was too badly damaged to be worth recovering.

Thus ended the Air Yacht. By this time, any hopes of a military role for it were well past, yet this unique Supermarine aircraft did look forward eight years to the Saunders-Roe A33. This aircraft, another 90ft parasol monoplane with similar supporting struts from its sponsons, was built in 1938, but the old porpoising problem caused structural failure of the mainplane on the first high speed taxiing test and it was not proceeded with.

Had Mitchell lived long enough, and had the Air Ministry generally shown a more single-minded faith in the future of monoplane flying boats, one wonders if Mitchell's last flying boat, the Stranraer biplane, would have been a Supermarine Air Yacht type equivalent to the American Catalina which equipped twenty-one RAF and Royal Canadian Air Force (RCAF) squadrons during the Second World War. Incidentally, the actual predecessor of the Catalina was the Consolidated Commodore, mentioned earlier as being aerodynamically far less clean than the Supermarine Air Yacht.

The Seamew

For the sake of completeness, the Seamew ought to be mentioned. Its first flight was in the year following that of the Nanok, and it also proved to be a disappointment. It had been designed as a three-man deck-landing reconnaissance seaplane and Mitchell decided on a twin-engined approach, even though it had about the same wingspan as his Seagull, Scarab and Sea Eagle machines. These single-engined designs, especially the ones with rear facing airscrews, were less affected by spray than the Seamew, where smaller propellers had to be substituted in order to counteract rapid deterioration due to water ingestion.

However, this expedient resulted in a reduced rate of climb, and the aircraft was also found to be very nose heavy and suffering from extensive corrosion to the type of metal being used in the airframe, as well as in the mainplane fittings. Two prototypes were built but they did not lead to any orders.

GIANTS

While the early Dornier Wal series had had a very obvious effect on the design of the Air Yacht, the huge Mark X version made a great impression in wider aviation circles when it arrived at Calshot in November 1930, for a two week stay. This version had a crew of ten and was capable of carrying seventy passengers, in something approaching steamship luxury. This included a smoking room with its own bar, a dining salon, and seating for the sixty-six passengers which could also be converted to sleeping berths for night flights. It was powered by twelve 610hp engines, accessible via a passageway in the wings.

The Type 179 Giant

Not entirely to be outdone, in 1929 the Air Ministry sent Supermarine a specification for a forty seat civil flying boat, which was first projected as a high-winged monoplane, with three fins, a relatively flat-sided fuselage and with bulbous floats attached to the underside of each wing root, bulky enough to be almost classified as sponsons. Six engines were to be mounted in tandem on pylons above the wing, Dornier X fashion and, notably, it had provision for passenger seating in the leading edge of the very thick wing.

While the new design was essentially a development from the Air Yacht, the former plank-shaped wing was now replaced by the first appearance of Supermarine elliptical flying surfaces. Its proposed torsion-resisting nose section also looked towards the wing structure of the Spitfire, as did the use of a single spar – although in this case it was to be 6ft in depth.

Had Mitchell's design been completed, its size would certainly have put his company ahead of other large flying boat contenders. It was to have a wingspan 65ft more than the contemporary six-engined Short Sarafand and nearly 3ft more than that of the imposing Dornier X. About this time, there was another very large, seven-engined aircraft – the K-7 designed by Constantin Kalinin – which, interestingly, also featured an early example of the elliptical wing (see the drawing on p.150). It should, however, be pointed out that, while the Russian plane has always attracted the attention of air historians because of its size (and because it flew), Mitchell's projected machine would have had a wingspan that was larger by 10ft. With a span of 185ft, its name 'Giant' was therefore appropriate, and it would have represented a significant departure from the previous, almost universal, formula of braced, fabric-covered biplanes.

Almost a year later, the rather untidy arrangement of three rows of forward facing engines was revised, whereby two inner nacelles now housed two engines apiece, facing fore and aft, and two outer nacelles had a single engine each, driving a tractor propeller. Rolls-Royce steam-cooled engines were now proposed, with the leading edge of the wing to be used as a steam condenser for the cooling system, a variation on the wing-surface radiator system of the S5 and S6 types. The passenger accommodation in the wings was to be eliminated in order to accommodate the evaporative cooling system, and this allowed the wing to have a thinner, more efficient, cross section. Mitchell had also decided upon a return to conventional wing-tip floats instead of the high-drag sponson type arrangement.

Thus by early 1931, when the keel of the Giant was laid down, most of the Dornier X influence had disappeared, as a company publicity photograph revealed (below).

While the early proposals for the Giant showed a tentative move forward, the upswept tail section, the nicely streamlined engine nacelles and the fore part of the hull now reveal Mitchell's thinking to be in advance of forthcoming larger American flying boats. For example, the Sikorsky S-40, of the same year that the keel of the Giant was laid down, represents a traditional approach of struts and wires; also, the 'canoe' hull and the necessary twin booms for the tail section, which no doubt achieved a good weight/strength ratio, did not represent the way forward for later flying boat designs (see drawing on p.81).

A graphic illustration of Supermarine's forward thinking (compare the Southampton, bottom left, on the Supermarine slipway). (Courtesy of Solent Sky Museum)

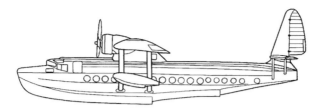

The Sikorsky S-42.

The later Sikorsky S-42 had a tail unit integral with the main fuselage, and had lost most of its predecessor's struts and wires. Coming a few years later than the proposed Giant, it had its engines neatly faired into the wing. It did, however, still retain wing and tailplane struts – compared with the Mitchell's projected cantilever structures – and this in a machine that was to have a wing-span of 185ft, compared with the 118ft span of the American aircraft.

Alas, early in 1932, the project was cancelled in view of the continued economic problems that faced the country, leaving Joe Smith, the chief draughtsman, the unpleasant task of laying off twenty of his drawing office staff. Consternation was not limited to Supermarine, for questions were asked in Parliament, where the Under Secretary for Air justified the government's decision, claiming that over 70 per cent of the estimated cost would be saved by cancellation. (Incidentally, nor had the Germans felt justified in putting their huge Do X into quantity production.)

Had the Giant been built, perhaps Mitchell's bomber (see pp.162 foll.) might have been designed earlier and might even have been in the air when the critical need arose for such weapons.

Meanwhile, one British aircraft of a somewhat similar type did actually fly. This was the Blackburn Sydney, a monoplane with a metal-skinned wing, albeit braced and of only 100ft span. This machine could also have spearheaded the movement away from the traditional British fabric-covered biplane, but the Air Ministry did not place a production order. It was thus fated that, owing to circumstances outside the control of Supermarine, Mitchell would not be remembered (as might otherwise have been predicted) for his contribution to the main flowering of the Imperial Airways routes, nor for the creation of later equivalents of the well-known wartime monoplane flying boats, the Sunderland and the Catalina.

MITCHELL'S SEAPLANES AT WAR

Most of Mitchell's seaplanes were designed for military purposes, although naval reconnaissance rather than bombing had been the main requirements from the Air Ministry. Foreign orders were more specifically aggressive:

the Scarab amphibian bomber for Spain and the Nanok torpedo carrier for Denmark. All the aircraft were, basically, traditional biplanes and Mitchell was also to design two other military biplane flying boats, closer to the outbreak of the Second World War, despite the obsolescence of their configuration.

The Scapa

The first of the new designs, which was to become known as the Scapa, was ordered as a successor to the long-serving Southampton, to be supplied with a metal hull and superstructure and with the new Rolls-Royce Kestrel engines. In the relatively depressed economic situation in Britain and with other companies offering multi-engined flying boats, a more aerodynamically efficient version of the Southampton with the cheapness of using only two of the new, efficient engines seemed a good proposition, and so Supermarine offered the last Southampton, S1648, as the proposed prototype, without extra cost to the Air Ministry.

The new aircraft was designated the Southampton IV and so it might have been regarded as, essentially, an 'improved Southampton', particularly as its water-planing lines resembled that of the previous aircraft. Indeed, tank testing now available via the new parent firm, Vickers, did not suggest any real need to depart from the earlier basic shape – a compliment to the intuitive design of the hull of 1925. In fact, a widening behind the step, to counteract spray hitting the tail surfaces, was abandoned when it was found to produce an unpleasant pitching on take-off.

In other respects, the new machine was, effectively, a new design. 'Stretching' the Southampton with a lengthened bow and a deeper forefoot, allied to a flatter top-decking, allowed for more useable space within, as well as significantly altering the appearance of the new machine. Also, the slab-sided approach of the Air Yacht and of the slightly later Walrus (another reflection of the economic situation?) was evident, although the upward sweep of the tail and other curvatures restored something of the elegance of the Southampton hull.

The superstructure was even more clearly a departure. The redesign meant that the sweep back of the mainplane outer sections, in response to the changing service loads of later Southamptons, was no longer necessary and the earlier two-bay structure and warren girders were now reduced to a much simpler arrangement, whereby two of the four struts also supported the engines. These engines were now positioned directly under the top wing and the previous triple fins were now succeeded by two units with extended rudders.

Beverley Shenstone, Mitchell's aerodynamicist, considered the resulting aircraft 'perhaps the cleanest biplane flying boat ever built, with minimum struttage and clean nacelles faired into the wing'. He did not mention the very 'boxy' radiators which projected on either side to the rear of these nacelles,

The Scapa prototype. (Courtesy of E.B. Morgan)

although this positioning least compromised the overall lines of the new design (see photograph above).

The new prototype made its first flight on 8 July 1932, and it was delivered at the end of October to the Marine Aircraft Experimental Establishment, Felixstowe, for service testing. In the following May, the prototype was flown to Malta, for overseas acceptance trials with No. 202 Squadron and these included a long-distance flight to Gibraltar and a cruise to Port Sudan via Sollum, Aboukir, and Lake Timsah. On its return, the Scapa took part in the 1934 fly-past of 'the competition' at the Hendon RAF display with, as Penrose reported, 'the clean Supermarine twin-engined Scapa leading, followed by the four-engined Short Singapore, triple engined Blackburn Perth, the distinctive gull-winged Short Knuckleduster, Saro R24/31 London and the three Saro Cloud trainers'.

The Hendon event was clearly designed to impress foreign governments with Britain's military capabilities and, during the 1936–1939 period, the Scapa fulfilled its required purpose with anti-submarine patrols to protect neutral shipping during the Spanish Civil War. Some of the aircraft of No. 202 squadron were later transferred to No. 204 Squadron and were sent to Egypt during the Italian–Abyssinian confrontation. There was also a single Scapa, attached to No. 228 Squadron, whose contribution to developing war preparations was its involvement in early radar trials.

The Stranraer

Soon after Supermarine had received orders for the Scapa, the Air Ministry issued another specification which was unlikely to be matched by a simple development of this last type. This latest specification was for another general purpose coastal patrol flying boat, of robust and simple construction with low maintenance costs, but capable of carrying a 1,000lb greater load and of maintaining height on one engine with 60 per cent of fuel on board.

An enlarged and substantially altered version of the Scapa had to be projected and a specification was submitted, alongside one from Shorts and one from Saunders-Roe. Only the last, the A27 London, was accepted and it was later ordered to replace the Southamptons and Scapas of Nos 201 and 202 Squadron respectively. The Short Singapore III had also been ordered as a replacement for other Scapas with Nos 204 and 240 Squadrons.

This Short machine had about the same speed as the Scapa and was powered by twice as many engines, and another Short machine, the Saraband, was only a few mph faster with six engines. Thus, given an economic situation in which orders for these larger flying boats were likely to be kept to a minimum, it seemed a distinct possibility that a performance from Mitchell's smaller, twin-engined proposal, if significantly better than that of the Saunders-Roe London, might still stand a chance of winning some contracts, given the growing calls for British rearmament.

Another reason for anticipating orders for the proposed new design was not simply based on the good performance figures that the Scapa had returned but on Mitchell's having come to believe in the virtue of employing a thin wing – for other than Schneider Trophy racers – contrary to the generally perceived wisdom of the day. The eventual outcome was an Air Ministry contract for a flying boat that outclassed all of its contemporaries of similar configuration.

The engines chosen initially to pull the new machine's thinner aerofoil through the air, and to give it the one-engine performance required by the Air Ministry specification, were 820hp Bristol Pegasus IIIMs, providing an additional 590hp more than the Scapa's Kestrels. These two engines were to be mounted with the same thrust line and in streamlined fairings but, being air-cooled radials, they did not incur the weight and drag penalties of the Scapa's radiators. Long-chord Townend drag-reducing rings now surrounded the cylinder heads and their oil coolers formed part of the top centre-section leading edge. Against these improvements, there was the additional 12 per cent increase in wing area of the new machine. This extra drag and weight was added to by the two-bay strut arrangement required to support the extra 10ft of wingspan that was needed to meet the new specification's load carrying requirements.

The larger size, nevertheless, did have some aerodynamic advantages. The extra depth of the hull allowed the top of the enclosed cockpit to form a continuous line with the midships gunner's cockpit, which was now placed in the centre of the hull top (in the Southampton and Scapa there had been two

The Stranraer prototype. (Courtesy of RAF Museum)

mid-ship gunner's cockpits, offset from the centre line). Now, for the first time, Supermarine had built a larger service aircraft which made it possible to install the second rear gunner more sensibly, in a faired-in cockpit in the tail. This had been proposed for the unsuccessful Vickers/Southampton X prototype, with its wingspan of 79ft, and so presented little difficulty for the new 85ft craft. Its 'general purpose' character was evidenced by the fitting of carriers below the inner sections of the lower wings for up to four 250lb bombs or extra fuel tanks. The flatter fuselage section between the lower wings was even more convenient than that of the Scapa for transporting supplies, such as a spare engine.

By the time that the designing and the constructing of the new prototype was well under way, the Australian Seagull V order had not yet been completed and the Scapa flying boat contract was also being fulfilled. Nevertheless, the new prototype, K3973, was test flown by Summers on 27 July 1934 and delivered in very short time to the Marine Aircraft Experimental Establishment at Felixstowe, for service assessment.

The performance of the aircraft was such that an order for seventeen aircraft, K7287–K7303, was placed with Supermarine by the following year. The standard service machine was fitted with the more powerful 920hp Pegasus X engines, giving it a maximum speed of 165mph and making it the fastest biplane flying boat to enter RAF service – yet with a stalling speed of only 51mph.

Its maximum ceiling was 20,000ft and it could climb to the first 10,000ft in ten minutes – the Scapa had taken twice as long, two years earlier. As it had been necessary to withhold these performance details because of the developing international situation, company publicity had to be content with the by-no-means despairing comment that the aircraft 'passed all its tests brilliantly' and went on to claim that:

> The outstanding feature of this flying boat is that the performance obtained during a series of extended service trials, whether in respect of speed, climb, ceiling or take-off, is unequalled by any other British flying boat. All the specification requirements were exceeded by large margins.

As the new aircraft had become quite distinct from the earlier Scapa from which it was developed, a new name was chosen and the machine entered service as the 'Stranraer'. It must have been gratifying for Supermarine to see the Saunders-Roe London flying boat then replaced by their new aircraft with Nos 201 and 240 Squadrons, and to see another rival company's aircraft, the Singapore III, superseded by the Stranraer with No. 209 Squadron. Other machines replaced the company's own Scapas with No. 228 Squadron and so the total of Stranraers ordered from Supermarine, including the prototype, came to eighteen.

It thus came about that the Stranraer was actually operated in the Second World War, serving with No. 228 Squadron, when it was needed to patrol the North Sea. Additionally, some of the Stranraers of this unit were transferred to No. 209 Squadron and, fitted with extra fuel tankage under one wing and bombs under the other, they conducted patrols against enemy shipping between Scotland and Norway, until replaced in April 1941 by the ubiquitous Short Sunderland. No. 240 Squadron was also equipped with the Stranraer and made the last operational patrol of the type on 17 March 1941, after which it was replaced by the American-built Catalina.

In addition to the British Stranraers, the Royal Canadian Air Force also adopted them; forty were built by Canadian Vickers and these saw a great deal more service than their British counterparts – in the battle against the U-boats in the Atlantic. The last RCAF Stranraer was retired as late as 20 January 1946, and fourteen of the aircraft were sold to the civil sector, particularly to private airline companies in Canada where the lakes of the Northern Territory provided ready-made runways. The last of the Stranraers served in these regions until 1958.

However, the longevity and performance of the Stranraer does not conceal the fact that, in this larger flying boat category, the influence of Mitchell was relatively short-lived – in many ways, a result of the lack of official encouragement for his Air Yacht (monoplane) approach to the reconnaissance flying boat type and of the cancellation of the Type 179 Giant cantilever monoplane.

Meanwhile, the early and single-minded approach of Shorts to all-metal aircraft had paid dividends and finally led to the military development of another cantilever monoplane type, the Sunderland, which dominated the wartime long-range sea patrol provision, with a total of 741 being built. In addition, Short's clean, streamlined civilian version had monopolised the flying boat provision on the Imperial Airways routes just prior to the outbreak of the war and represented a major step forward in flying boat design, without a rival aircraft from Supermarine.

'HE LOOPED THE BLOODY THING!'

After the Spitfire, the Walrus is probably the best-known RAF aircraft to come from Mitchell's drawing board. Yet it owed its origin to an Australian order for a replacement for the Supermarine Seagull IIIs, which the Royal Australian Air Force had been operating since 1926 (including an annual race between these staid machines at a regatta in Hervey Bay, north of Brisbane).

The Seagull V/Walrus

In 1930, an Australian specification had been sent around British aircraft firms for a replacement reconnaissance amphibian which could be catapulted with full military load, and which was also capable of shipboard stowage. In view of the deck-landing limitations and porpoising characteristics of their aging Seagull III, the Seagull V, as the Australian aircraft was to be named, had to be a complete redesign for reasons other than obsolescence (the earliest version of the type, the Seal, first flew in 1921).

In fact, it might be fairly accurate to say that the only influence of the older type on the Seagull V was the basic layout of the last experimental Seagull II, N9644, a biplane amphibian which had reverted to the use of a pusher air-cooled power unit. Otherwise, the move to metal structures, slab-sided fuselages, and the experience of the intervening years, produced a quite distinct type within the older formula.

One significant aspect of the redesign was the employment of a fully retracting undercarriage, which had featured little in Air Ministry requirements – although, as we have seen, Mitchell had had to invent mechanisms since 1920 to lift his amphibians' wheels out of the water. Now, Alan Clifton persuaded Mitchell to retract the wheels into the wing, saying 'We shall have to do it eventually, why not now?'

Another aspect of the redesign was the hull. It now displayed the slab-sided features of the Scapa and the later Stranraer, but without their upward sweep to the tail unit and with a one-step planning surface. Various reasons contributed to the especially utilitarian appearance to the hull, but the foremost need inherent in Mitchell's redesign was to improve on the 'sea state' performance of the Seagull III.

Supermarine's move to metal structures would contribute to the sturdiness of the proposed Seagull V, signified by the direct attachment of the lower wings to the hull, as the new material would be less prone to failure at the join. Again, this feature was similar to that in the recent Scapa, and the Stranraer that followed, although in this case there was no elegant lower wing centre-section and the upper centre-section was functionally cut back for clearance of the propeller, and cut back again to allow for wing folding. But then, speed was not a requisite in a ship's aircraft where spotting would be one of its main functions. On the other hand, the lower wing did not have the large cut-outs of its predecessors, as the inner portion of the wing behind the rear spar could be folded away in order to clear the hull sides for stowage; and the wings had single bay struts similar to the recent Seamew and Scapa designs.

Compared with these other two seaplanes, the new design overall had a much more 'minimalist' appearance which was not decreased by the engine having the traditional Supermarine position between the wings, supported by eight struts, and by its nacelle being noticeably offset to counteract the corkscrew pressure of the propeller slipstream on one side of the fin.

The new machine was clearly no beauty and its functional appearance, allied with its very traditional configuration, appeared to have won it no friends when, in June 1933, the prototype was completed and seen by the Air Ministry Director of Technical Development. Those at Supermarine with long memories

The Seagull V prototype on Southampton Water. (Courtesy of Solent Sky Museum)

of the inability of the company to win orders for their naval amphibian fighter type could hardly have been encouraged by the director's comment to Clifton: 'Very interesting; but of course we have no requirement for anything like this.'

Perhaps this reaction had some bearing on the test pilot's performance at the 1933 SBAC Show at Hendon. *The Aeroplane* nicely described the event:

> This boat made its maiden flight on 21 June, five days before its first public appearance, but Mr Summers proved its qualities by throwing it about in a most carefree manner. Of its performance little is known but there can be little doubt about its amiability and general handiness in the air and on the ground. One must be prepared to see all sorts of aeroplanes looping and rolling with abandon nowadays, but somehow one has, up to now, looked to the flying boat to preserve that Victorian dignity which one associates with crinolines, side whiskers, bell-bottom trousers and metal hulls. The Seagull V destroyed all one's illusions.

Henry Knowler, chief designer at Saunders-Roe, who watched the display in the company of Mitchell, reported the designer's understandable surprise and anxiety at the low-level antics of the five-day old prototype. 'He looped the bloody thing!' Mitchell kept repeating to everyone he met.

He had obviously not heard that a disgruntled American pilot had once done the same over Killingholme in a 95ft Felixstowe flying boat. Nor did he live to see the production of the Walrus (its later British name) as flown by Supermarine test pilot George Pickering:

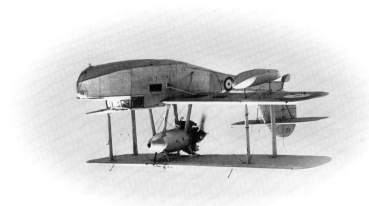

At the finish of the test he would fly very low over the river, by low I mean about 300ft or so, in front of the flight shed and loop the Walrus to signal that it had passed the test; if not, he would just land and return up the slip and it would be worked upon. If you haven't seen a Walrus looped, you haven't lived. [As recounted by Peter Weston, who began his varied flying career as a Supermarine apprentice in 1938.]

Thereafter, the Seagull V underwent modifications and trials. Test pilot 'Mutt' Summers criticised the rigidity of the undercarriage and the lack of steering capacity on the ground, and these deficiencies had had to be put right. By this time it had been discovered that another make of aircraft had been allocated its N1 number, so the one-and-only Supermarine prototype now became N2 and went to the MAEE on 29 July, just over six weeks after its maiden flight. Evaluation tests then lasted until the end of October, after which the Seagull went to the Royal Aircraft Establishment at Farnborough for the catapulting trials required by the Australian Government.

Now the empty weight of the aircraft had gone up to 5,016lb and Mitchell, having returned to work at the end of 1933 after his operation for cancer, ordered an aerodynamic clean-up as parasitic drag had appreciably reduced the performance of the heavier machine.

Despite the lengthy testing, including successful catapult trials, no British order was expected. Webb, now in the business manager's department, quoted an Air Ministry letter, saying that 'we do not envisage any role for an aircraft of this type with HM Forces'. He also relates how serving officers at the nearby flying boat base at Calshot could also see no use for it. One of them asked, 'What are you people doing wasting our time on a machine like that – it will be shot out of the skies by the fighters?' So Webb pointed out that there would be no fighters with enough range to shoot anything down in mid-ocean and that, catapulted from a cruiser or battleship, it would be the eyes of the fleet.

The aircraft was then taken back to home waters for the continuation of trials at Sheerness and in the Solent until May, when it was returned to Supermarine for the fitting of redesigned wing-tip floats for improved buoyancy, the removal of the wheel brakes for lightness and for an improved layout of the observer's compartment.

Further fleet operation trials continued, including 'sea state' landings in 30 knot winds and 6ft waves off the Kyles of Bute, and underway recovery onto a warship making up to 13 knots through rough water. In these trials the Royal Navy had been acting as 'programme manager' for the Australians and, as a result, their government ordered twenty-four production Seagull Vs, A2-1 through to A2-24.

Thus it would appear that the future of Mitchell's design would rest solely with the Australian Government's requirement, but movements were afoot nearer to home, as reported in Caspar John's foreword to *The Supermarine Walrus*:

> To the late Rear Admiral Maitland W.S. Boucher DSO, Royal Navy [at that time serving in the Naval Air Division], goes the initiative for the introduction to the Fleet Air Arm of this somewhat improbable looking, yet highly successful flying machine.
>
> He said to me one day in late 1933, 'I've just been to Supermarines. I've seen a small amphibian. It looks handy, tough and versatile … something the navy needs. I want you to put it through its service trials. Off you go.' With a Supermarine Southampton flying boat course at Calshot and some tests at Felixstowe intervening, off I went to Woolston to collect Seagull V N2 early in 1934.

Caspar John, son of the artist Augustus John and later Admiral of the Fleet, took the Seagull to Gibraltar for rough weather take-offs and landings and for fleet co-operation exercises, after which it was described as 'the complete answer to our prayers'.

Thereafter, N2 was purchased by the Air Ministry, renumbered K4797, and on New Year's Day 1935 it was handed over to the Fleet Air Arm for a short series of official acceptance trials. As the prototype had first flown in June 1933, it is clear that the Admiralty had needed some time to be convinced that open sea and catapult operation from their capital ships would work smoothly. No doubt the Australian initiative helped to overcome any doubters, and an initial British order was placed on 18 May for twelve aircraft.

The first machine of the 1934 Australian order flew on 25 June 1935, and after a further eleven had been completed, the Air Ministry took delivery of their first batch. The rest of the Australian order was then completed, along with a second batch of eight for the Air Ministry, and the developing international situation then contributed to a much larger order for twenty-eight.

A name was now to be chosen for the British machine, unlike those for Australia which retained the Seagull V appellation. In the past, Supermarine amphibians had been favoured mainly with 'nice' seabird names: Sea Eagle, Seagull, Sheldrake, Seamew, and so on, while the name Sea Lion was a nod in the direction of the engine used. It is an interesting comment on this latest amphibian's 'somewhat improbable' appearance that the far less glamorous name 'Walrus' was now chosen.

Nevertheless, it was not only the first British aircraft to be catapulted with a full military load but it was also the first British designed military aircraft with a retracting undercarriage. Only a few months earlier, Admiral Sir Roger Backhouse had received a ducking when the prototype Walrus, being used as his 'barge', was landed in the sea with the undercarriage still down and turned turtle. After that, the Walrus was fitted with a horn to warn pilots of what was then a novel feature.

The original batches of forty-eight aircraft ordered for the navy was increased dramatically in 1936 with the requirement for another 168 machines. Despite its initially very doubtful future and its backwards-looking appearance, the Walrus became the last and the most successful of all Mitchell's reconnaissance amphibians and the navy's standard wartime fleet spotter.

⑦

PERSPECTIVES ON THE SPITFIRE

John Shelton

BRITISH FIGHTERS BEFORE THE SPITFIRE

In order to appreciate the significant advance in design represented by Mitchell's Spitfire, it is necessary to look back at the RAF fighters that came before it. The aircraft of the two decades after the end of the First World War were, almost without exception, biplanes with fixed undercarriages and powered by radial, air-cooled engines. However, the drag penalty of this type of machine, with its attendant struts and wires, began to have an increasingly inhibiting effect on performance. The drag of a particular airframe increases exponentially in relation to an increase in its speed – to double an aircraft's speed would, theoretically, require four times its engine power (see the table on p.147, which includes details of the gradually increasing discrepancy between increases in engine power and speed in aircraft of this period).

One notable exception to the general pattern of fighter development was the Hawker Fury which, in 1931, showed a 16 per cent speed increase over the Bristol Bulldog for only 7 per cent more power – the result, in particular, of using a closely cowled, in-line, water-cooled engine. The Hawker Hornet, its predecessor, had already shown the advantage of such a power unit, but the new Air Ministry specification, F.7/30, gave no specific steer towards any particular engine configuration – contrary to the impression given by the employment of the in-line Rolls-Royce Goshawk engine in five of the competing designs, including Mitchell's.

The Gloster Gamecock, which entered squadron service in 1926, had a top speed of 155mph and the Bristol Bulldog of 1929 was only about 20mph faster – an average increase of about 7mph per year. Thus, in 1931, when the Air Ministry released its new fighter requirement, no more than, say, 185mph might be expected if manufacturers responded to the new specification with the usual biplane configuration, air-cooled radial engine, and fixed undercarriage. It can therefore be seen that F.7/30, which was issued for the replacement of the Bulldog and which eventually led to the Spitfire, represented a significant challenge (although tempered by realism) to an unadventurous aircraft industry. The new type was required to have a top speed of 'not less than 195mph' while carrying double the number of guns.

The RAF had begun large-scale air exercises in 1927 and, as a result, it was appreciated how the biplane formula limited the fighter pilot's view of 'invading' bombers. In this respect, the F.7/30 requirement was quite specific: 'the pilot must have a clear view forward and upward' and 'particular care is needed to prevent his view of hostile aircraft being blanked out by top planes and centre sections'.

PREVIOUS: The Spitfire prototype and Type 224. (From paintings by the author)

One suspects a strong hint that monoplane prototypes might be welcome, but it is a reflection of the 1930 design scene that only three of the eventual eight entries were not biplanes. Mitchell's machine was, unsurprisingly, a monoplane, but the only aircraft that was submitted with a retracting undercarriage was not his. Again, there had been no specific Ministry requirement in this respect.

It might be that certain omissions or limitations of F.7/30 are more obvious in hindsight, but it is still evident that it was something of a milestone in Ministry thinking, that it was feeling its way towards a new approach to fighter design. In summary, the specification called for a four-gun, single-seat day and night fighter with manoeuvrability and a 'fighting view', a speed of not less than 195mph at 15,000ft, a landing speed not more than 60mph, and a climb to 15,000ft in eight and a half minutes. Satisfying this 1930 requirement was unlikely to be easily achieved, especially as a low landing speed consideration for a night fighter might very well inhibit the design of a high speed machine otherwise dedicated to daytime flying.

Additionally, the choice of the new water-cooled, in-line, Goshawk engine did not help despite being predicted to produce 660hp (compared with the 450hp of the Bristol Jupiter VII radial engine of the Bulldog). This engine was designed to work with a new water cooling system, the so-called evaporative method, which was expected to bring with it significant reductions in drag – by not requiring conventional radiators to keep the engine coolant below boiling point. The water in the engine was kept under pressure by pumps, allowing it to heat to temperatures above 100°C and then the superheated water was released to turn to steam in a suitable container, with sides exposed to the airflow, where it would condense on cooling and be returned to the engine. The greater efficiency of this cooling method would therefore require an aircraft to carry less water and could operate via, and under, the skin of the aircraft, resulting in a zero-drag cooling system.

In practice, it was found that the steam condensers of the F.7/30 Westland entry could not cope with varying flight and atmospheric conditions, and the Blackburn prototype exceeded maximum temperatures within a few minutes. Additionally, the latter had ground handling problems, caused by its high centre of gravity, and never flew, thus justifying the opinion of its test pilot, 'Dasher' Blake, that 'the little beast has no future'.

Two other prototypes powered by the Goshawk engine, the Hawker PV 3 and the Bristol Type 123, fared little better. Type 123 encountered initial cooling problems and was also laterally unstable and was withdrawn. The Hawker entry (essentially, a re-engined Fury) paid only a brief visit to Martlesham owing to its unsatisfactory cooling system. (The similar cooling problems which dogged Mitchell's Type 224 entry will be discussed in the next chapter.)

There were other disappointments. The top speed of the Westland entry was only 146mph and it took nearly nineteen minutes to reach 20,000ft (in appearance, it had some similarities with the company's army co-operation Lysander, especially in the cockpit area, but this was hardly a recommendation for a fighter proposal). It would appear to have been unduly influenced by the F.7/30 concern for a good pilot position, as did the Blackburn entry, and like the Hawker and Bristol machines, both were basically conventional biplanes with fixed undercarriages.

Of the two monoplane rivals to Mitchell's Type 224 entry, the Vickers Type 151 Jockey was 10mph slower and proposals to re-engine it came to nothing when the sole prototype was lost to a flat spin in June 1932. But at least the other monoplane might very well have attracted favourable Ministry support, instead of the Spitfire. Bristol decided to improve upon its Type 123 entry by substituting the Goshawk for a Bristol Mercury engine. This new Type 133 was a considerable improvement on its predecessor in other ways: despite now having an air-cooled engine, it was the first proposed RAF fighter with retractable wheels, and its stressed-skin construction, employing the recently invented Alclad sheeting, allowed for the design of a forward-looking cantilever monoplane. Its test pilot, Cyril Uwins, was very impressed by its performance and the top speed of 260mph but, when the aircraft was almost ready to go for competitive tests at Martlesham Heath, it also entered into a flat spin which was irrecoverable and the test pilot had to abandon another one-and-only prototype.

The surviving monoplane entry, Mitchell's Type 224, ought to have had a competitive performance, thanks to Mitchell's obsessive concern to keep frontal area to a minimum and its being a cantilever monoplane, but, apart from the problematic evaporative cooling system, it had the greatest wingspan and therein lay its main problem – as will be seen next.

MITCHELL'S STUKA – THE FIRST SPITFIRE

Mitchell's engagement with the land-based fighter concept began almost at the same time as the last of his Schneider Trophy racers was built. Thus, Mitchell's qualifications for creating high speed aircraft were outstanding but, as we shall see, much of the under-performance of his first attempt at a fighter was not of Mitchell's making. Equally, its genesis contradicts any assumption that the Spitfire developed directly from his Schneider Trophy machines or rose by some single conceptual leap after the designer returned to work at the end of 1933, following his operation for cancer.

As it was, in 1931 when the Ministry specification appeared, Mitchell had had to turn his mind to a military aspect of aviation that he had only briefly been engaged upon with the Sea King II of 1921 – and that aircraft was a flying boat, albeit a fast and manoeuvrable one at the time. Additionally, armament on his slower reconnaissance flying boats was provided via gunners in cockpits not via guns which would now probably need to be buried in the wings.

Alan Clifton recalled that Mitchell was uneasy about 'his first venture into military aircraft', recognising that he was 'no expert in the field'. Thus, with typical pragmatism, he asked 'Mutt' Summers, Vickers' chief test pilot, to arrange a visit to the Martlesham test centre to find out what RAF pilots considered to be most important in a fighting machine.

Type 224

Mitchell's resultant design, Type 224, was an all-metal structure with a thick cantilever, inverted, gull wing and a short fixed undercarriage with large fairings (hence the comparison with the Junkers Stuka – see below).

Supermarine's submission to the Air Ministry pointed out how this cranked wing configuration would produce a short, low drag undercarriage with a wide track for easy taxiing, and give 'exceptional' visibility for the pilot. An inverted gull wing and fixed undercarriage configuration meant that the latter would be reasonably short and light and would also help to satisfy the F.7/30 armament requirement – two of the four guns could be housed in the undercarriage fairings (the leading edges of the wings were to incorporate radiators for the evaporative engine cooling system). In addition, tanks to collect the condensed water coolant could be fitted low down in these fairings.

A large air brake was employed which could be lowered from the underside of the fuselage but nevertheless the Air Ministry, concerned about night operation and small, grass field landing strips, felt that the estimated wing loading of only 15lb per sq. ft was too high (Mitchell's S6B loading had been 42lbs per sq. ft).

Type 224, at the 1934 RAF display, Hendon. (Courtesy of E.B. Morgan)

Therefore, the wing was eventually drawn up with a generous 45ft 10in span which, in combination with a fuselage about the same length as that of the 28ft 10in span Schneider floatplane, looked somewhat out of proportion.

Type 224 first flew on 19 February 1933 and, unfortunately, it was found that the low pressure side of the pumps for the cooling system would often allow the coolant to turn into steam again, particularly during rapid climbs. (Mitchell's early apprenticeship to a locomotive manufacturer did not include high-altitude problems!) Jeffrey Quill has recorded how he did not exactly please the chief designer when he commented on the situation:

> I said that with the red [warning] lights flashing on all over the place, one had to be a plumber to understand what was going on. He didn't say anything, he just looked very sour. He was rather sensitive about the aeroplane and obviously I had trodden on his toes.

Mitchell, understandably, was less than pleased when the pilot had to level off until all was working normally again, thus defeating the F.7/30 requirement of the fastest possible climb to intercept enemy bombers.

Apart from the cooling problems, the top speed of Type 224 also proved to be a disappointment and so, when Mitchell returned to work after his operation, modifications were proposed, including a retractable undercarriage, and elimination of the cranked wing. These proposals were submitted in July 1934 and were expected to improve the maximum speed of Type 224 by 30mph, but none were implemented and no further prototype was ordered.

The Junkers Ju 87B Stuka with early 'trousered' undercarriage.

Test flying continued, and Vickers even named the aircraft 'Spitfire', but the way forward was unlikely to be with an unsatisfactory cooling system and with the conflicting Ministry requirements of slow speed landing performance and fighter agility.

Meanwhile, Junkers were producing the similarly configured Stuka. Because it was designed as a two-seater, the German machine had a much larger cockpit canopy but it notably featured an inverted cranked wing and fixed under-carriage; in the case of the early models, the wheels were similarly encased (see photograph opposite). It first flew on 17 September 1935 and, a year later, Blohm und Voss produced their Ha137, a fighter type which also had a cranked wing and a 'trousered' undercarriage.

This similarity can also be seen in the Kawasaki Ki-5 – not surprisingly, as it came from the same designer. Like the Type 224, it first flew in February 1934, thus showing that there was nothing derivative or eccentric about Mitchell's basic approach, even if other factors had militated against it. The Japanese fighter had a span about 11ft shorter and, with over 200hp more, could reach 240mph – about 10mph faster than the Supermarine prototype. The Blohm and Voss Ha137 first flew thirteen months later and the in-line-engined ver-sions reached a maximum speed of 205mph with a 610hp engine. Again, the span was about 9ft less than that of the Type 224.

Despite Mitchell's disappointment with his fighter, it can be seen that its top speed of 228mph was actually quite creditable for its 600hp engine power, and the imposed penalty of the much larger wingspan – the other aircraft mentioned above averaged about 2ft longer than Type 224, while being about 7ft less in wingspan.

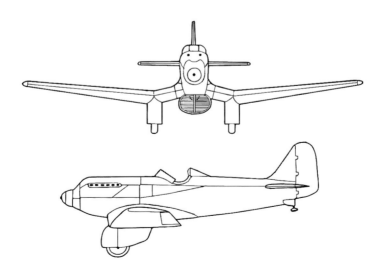

The Kawasaki Ki-5.

Thus, while Mitchell's chosen configuration of a cranked wing and a short fixed undercarriage was not an eccentric choice, nor derived from other aircraft, the landing speed restriction must have been one of the main reasons why the Vickers chairman instructed Mitchell to design a private venture aircraft, the future Spitfire, without any 'interference' from the Air Ministry (see next).

THE REAL SPITFIRE – A CLOSE RUN THING

Despite Mitchell's success in the final three Schneider Trophy contests, it had begun to appear that Supermarine might not do equally well in producing a winning land plane fighter.

For example, when Mitchell's first fighter design, the Type 224 'Spitfire', was failing to satisfy the Air Ministry F.7/30 specification, there was the other machine of forward-looking design which might very well have attracted favourable Ministry support instead. The Bristol Type 133 was another monoplane and was also the first British fighter design with both retractable wheels and stressed-skin construction. It had a more streamlined sliding cockpit canopy and the wing roots were aerodynamically faired into the fuselage with fillets (which Mitchell had only experimented with during the later days of Type 224).

However, as mentioned previously, the one-and-only prototype crashed and so time was available for Supermarine to try to improve upon their proposal – although, in view of the British manufacturers' disappointing responses to F.7/30, there was even talk in the Ministry of purchasing Poland's all-metal monoplane, the PZL P24. This monoplane was faster than any of the British prototypes and many were equipped with the more impressive firepower of two cannons, as well as two machine guns.

But, at least, personnel were changing in the Air Ministry. The Chief of the Air Staff, Sir Hugh Trenchard, who had favoured concentration on the bomber as a deterrent, had retired and it was fortunate for Mitchell that the Air Ministry and its departments were headed by RAF officers who had by now come to the conclusion that it was fighter development that had to be significantly stepped up.

And so, even before trials of the other, largely unsuccessful, F.7/30 prototypes had been concluded, specification F.5/34 was issued, which now stated that a retracting undercarriage was required as well as eight machine guns to provide 'the maximum hitting power'. It also specified that 'the maximum speed at an altitude of 15,000ft shall not be less than 275mph and at 5,000ft not less than 250mph', and that 'the time taken to reach 20,000ft is not to exceed 7½ minutes'. As Mitchell's Type 224 modifications had only promised a top speed of 265mph and a climb to 15,000ft in over eight minutes, it was clear that Supermarine had to do some serious rethinking.

At this time, a new engine was being developed by Rolls-Royce, who had decided that the next generation of fighters would need a new engine. Something between their 21-litre Kestrel and Goshawk engines and their 37-litre Schneider Trophy 'R' engine had been proposed. It was designated PV12, where the initials stood for 'private venture' and clearly indicated another independent appreciation of the need for Britain to develop better aircraft.

This new engine passed its 100 hour test in the July of 1934, and the board of Vickers (Aviation) Ltd decided on 6 November to finance the design of a machine powered by this new engine. Sir Robert McLean, the chairman of the Vickers board, later described how he had decided that Mitchell and his design team should design a 'real killer fighter' in advance of any Air Ministry specification, and that 'in no circumstances would any technical member of the Air Ministry be consulted or allowed to interfere with the designer' – no doubt with the unhappy history of Type 224 in mind.

It has been recently revealed that the chairman had not, in fact, been unwavering before his support for the Supermarine designer finally won out. The alternative was the parent company's Venom, a development of the promising but ill-fated F.7/30 entry, the Type 151 Jockey, which had also succumbed to a flat spin. Like the Spitfire, the Venom had a stressed-skin cantilever wing, retractable undercarriage and a metal monocoque fuselage. In fact, when it did fly, three months after the Spitfire prototype, it attained a top speed only 37mph lower than the Supermarine prototype – and with a less powerful, radial engine.

Clearly, this machine could also have developed into a very serious challenge to the Supermarine project and, indeed, Beverley Shenstone, Mitchell's aerodynamicist, later reported that in his opinion the Spitfire would not have been born 'if Mitchell had not been willing to stand up to McLean, particularly in the era when McLean clearly preferred the Venom concept to the Spitfire concept because it was cheaper and lighter'.

Once Mitchell's proposal had overcome this hurdle, the combination of a Vickers/Supermarine/Rolls-Royce/Mitchell design must have stirred up the new blood within the Air Ministry, for events then moved very quickly. On 1 December £10,000 was allocated for Supermarine to build a prototype and, when a full design conference was called at the Air Ministry on the 5th of the same month, it was headed by Air Marshall Hugh Dowding.

The modifications to Type 224 proposed by Supermarine had been deemed too late and too extensive to qualify for re-entry into the F.7/30 exercise, but fortunately the Air Ministry, in their concern to improve the fighter breed, agreed to Supermarine proceeding independently with their new design and a special specification F.37/34 was drawn up and formally signed on 3 January 1935. It should be noted that this new specification was headed 'Experimental High Speed Single-Seat Fighter (Supermarine Aviation Works)' and it stated that, basically, 'the aircraft shall conform to all the requirements stated in specification F.7/30' – that is, Mitchell was to design a four-gun aircraft but without other firms being invited to tender in the usual way.

The word 'experimental' might very well have reflected decreasing confidence in Supermarine among Air Ministry officials after the experience of Type 224, or that the three successive Schneider Trophy wins by the Rolls-Royce/Supermarine combination had not been forgotten by the new Air Ministry officials and was used to deflect criticism that the normal method of aircraft procurement was being bypassed.

Whatever support there might have been for a Supermarine project, it was not lost on the company that Hawker had also been encouraged to substantially modify their Super Fury F.7/30 entry with a rival 'experimental' offering. The Air Ministry additionally issued F.10/35, three months after the Supermarine requirement, calling for at least six, and preferably eight, guns to 'produce the maximum hitting power possible in the short time available for one attack'. They also issued specification F.37/35, for a single-seat day and night fighter armed with four cannon.

The Westland response, the Whirlwind, when it first flew in 1938, would have been a formidable aircraft that might have soon replaced a Supermarine fighter. It had an extremely low frontal area, an excellent pilot view, a top speed of 360mph, and its four 20mm cannons promised to make it the most heavily armed fighter aircraft of its era. Also, as the armament was mounted in a nose cluster, there were no convergence problems as with wing-mounted guns.

Thus, the Supermarine fighter being designed would have to offer something special, for F.10/35 called for a maximum speed of 'not less than 310mph'. In the event, engine problems with the Whirlwind (and with the later Hurricane replacement, the Typhoon) left the field clear for Spitfire development. At the same time, one suspects that Supermarine and Vickers were looking well beyond their designated four-gun model, and towards the greater speed and armament requirements, when their elliptical wing shape was decided upon – the thin wing, which Mitchell had come to believe would give him the speed, would only accommodate any increased weaponry via the broad chord of an elliptical wing, given the need also to allow for a retracted undercarriage.

Clifton later recorded that Mitchell specified a wing that had a thickness/chord ratio of 13 per cent at the root and 6 per cent at the tip, although advised by the National Physical Laboratory that wind tunnel tests showed that there was no advantage in going below a thickness chord ratio of 15 per cent.

Fortunately Mitchell's instincts were proved correct when the Spitfire proto-type's top speed was eventually achieved.

It was also fortunate that, about this time, F.W. Meredith of the Royal Aircraft Establishment, Farnborough, had come up with a ducted underwing radiator that not only impacted less on the streamlines of a machine but actually used the heat exchange of the radiator to produce some thrust at high speed – thereby encour-aging confidence in Supermarine's predicted 350mph for their new fighter.

Nevertheless, when the new prototype first flew early in 1936, Mitchell had to acknowledge that the top speed was 'a lot slower than I had hoped for' – and as its test pilot, Jeffrey Quill, said, 'Unless the Spitfire offered some very substantial speed advantage over the Hurricane, it was unlikely to be put into production. Thus the disappointing speed performance of our prototype at that early stage was something of a crisis and Mitchell was a very worried man.'

The prototype was given a special new paint job and, by 9 May 1936, re-emerged with a very smooth light blue-grey finish, thanks to the application of fillers and automobile paint supplied by Rolls-Royce. Despite the smooth new finish, the speed of the aircraft was still less than hoped for (bearing in mind F.10/35) and the aircraft's top speed of 335mph was still thought to be too close to that of the Hurricane, which was believed to be around 330mph.

Fortunately, the fitting of a particular propeller (Quill mentioned flight test-ing 'some 15 to 20 different designs') on 15 May produced a very impressive speed increase to 349mph. The following chart, comparing performances with those of preceding aircraft, clearly shows the achievement that this new aircraft represented and the reason why it was ordered with such alacrity after its first service test at Martlesham:

Aircraft	Power	Top Speed	Power Increase	Speed Increase
Gamecock (1926)	425hp	155mph		
Bulldog II (1929)	440hp	178mph	3.5 per cent	15 per cent
Gauntlet (1936)	640hp	230mph	45 per cent	30 per cent
Gladiator (1937)	830hp	253mph	30 per cent	12 per cent
Spitfire Mk I (1938)	1079hp	362mph	24 per cent	41 per cent

It can be seen that the increase in top speeds from 1926 to 1937 was 98mph. Over the eleven years this averaged 9mph per year, and the Gladiator (which had eventually been awarded the F.7/30 contract) registered an increase of only 23mph for the 30 per cent power increase over the Gauntlet of the year before.

The Spitfire entered squadron service the following year with a power increase of less than 25 per cent and, instead of replicating the usual speed increase of less than 10mph per year, achieved ten times that figure. It is perhaps

Believed to have been taken during Mitchell's last airborne viewing of his fighter prototype.
(Courtesy of P. Jarrett)

not always appreciated that it was the initial order for the Spitfire which concentrated minds in Germany and led to the order for the Messerschmitt Bf.109
(see p.152).

When one remembers how two F.7/30 contenders were eliminated when
the one, and only, model crashed, it is worth recalling that the equally unique
Spitfire prototype nearly came to grief when handed over to Flight Lieutenant
(later Air Marshall Sir) Humphrey Edwardes-Jones at the Martlesham Heath
test centre. In his account to Price of his first landing, he confessed that
owing to a distraction he nearly forgot to lower the still novel undercarriage.
One wonders how a crash-landing of the sole untried prototype would have
affected its future, or at least its delivery, when being required for the Battle of
Britain. (For the German contract exercise, equivalent to the British F.7/30
requirement, four firms had each been authorised to build three prototypes.)

Events in Europe were certainly now creating an even greater urgency to
find an adequate replacement for the standard RAF fighters of the day and, after
the many doubts along the way, high hopes were now being felt for this latest
Rolls-Royce/Supermarine/Mitchell 'experimental' machine. Thus it was that
Edwardes-Jones' first flight took place, unusually, as soon as the aircraft had been
delivered to Martlesham. Additionally, the pilot was instructed to telephone the Air
Ministry as soon as he got down and report on its suitability for squadron pilots.

Eight days later, on the strength of that brief conversation, and just less
than three months since the prototype's first flight on 5 March 1936, the Air
Ministry signed a contract for the first 310 Spitfires.

THE SPITFIRE WING

The film about Mitchell, *The First of the Few*, shows him looking at seagulls, presumably for inspiration when contemplating his future fighter – had he been concerned with the sort of glider development going on in Germany at the time, a case might have been made for his apparent interest in such birds. His keeping racing pigeons during his youth was evidence of an interest in flight, no doubt, but – as Jeffrey Quill observed – Mitchell had better things to do when designing aircraft than 'looking at bloody seagulls'. One might perhaps note that his first foray into fighter design, Type 224, had a *gull* wing – but it was inverted, and every effort was made to avoid the current aerodynamic problems of 'flutter'!

Other assumptions that the legendary Spitfire was a direct development of his Schneider Trophy machines, or that it was conceived in some moment of inspiration following his operation for cancer, are also far from the truth – as reference to the changing proposals around this time will show. Supermarine drawing No. 300000, Sheet 2, shows how the Type 224 wingspan was reduced by nearly 10ft with an almost straight trailing edge and a swept-back, straight leading edge with a rearwards sloping main spar. Sheet 11 also shows a continuance of the main spar positioning, but a distinct movement towards the elliptically shaped wing that was to become, pre-eminently, the distinctive feature of the Spitfire.

The successor to Mitchell's first fighter design was, at first, still to be designed around the evaporation cooled Rolls-Royce Goshawk engine as, whatever the problems, it offered a considerable reduction in drag. Then, in October 1934, the Air Ministry suggested that the proposed fighter should be fitted with a Napier Dagger engine, expected to be more powerful than the Goshawk. But, Rolls-Royce had, by then, produced their PV12 engine and the board of Vickers decided to finance a design powered by the new engine – which was,

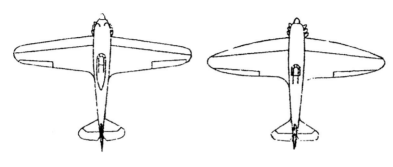

Sheet 2.

Sheet 11.

of course, to become the famous Merlin. As the new engine from Rolls-Royce was significantly heavier than the one that had been previously allowed for, it would need a less swept-back wing and so the eventual Spitfire wing shape became a modified ellipse, with a much straighter leading edge.

The Elliptical Wing

By this time, the elliptical wing was coming to be regarded as the most efficient shape for the sorts of speeds and altitudes that were now being contemplated. As Shenstone said, 'Aerodynamically it was the best for our purposes because the induced drag – that caused in producing lift – was lowest when this shape was used.' The Heinkel He.70 transport, which first flew in 1932, has sometimes been cited as influencing the Spitfire wing design, but such a transport aircraft was an unlikely model for the new breed of fighter, where climb, speed and manoeuvrability were paramount considerations. On the other hand, it did illustrate the appreciation that the elliptical wing was also a very efficient way of accommodating stress loads and hence of allowing a lighter structure.

The enormous Kalinin K-7 was being built at the same time and embodied, perhaps, the ultimate symmetrical elliptical wing to support its 174ft span and seven engines. But it should be remembered that its generic elliptical wing shape had been considered by Mitchell in connection with his 185ft Giant – projected before the Russian aircraft first flew. It is also worth mentioning that there was an earlier precedent for the elliptical wing approach – the two-seat light aircraft, the Bäumer Sausewind, notable for its all-cantilever structure as early as 1925. It was designed by the Günter brothers before they joined Heinkel and produced the above mentioned He70. Again, one finds that in that same year, Mitchell had also produced something approaching an elliptical wing with his S4 – which

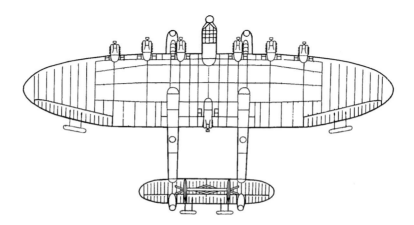

The Kalinin K-7.

also featured all-cantilever flying surfaces despite being required to withstand far greater loads than those of the German light aircraft.

The question arises: why did his S5/6 series of racers, which were the immediate forerunners of the Spitfire, not follow this precedent? It may very well be that, with the short development times available before the 1927–1931 competitions, the introduction of wing-surface radiators with the S5 was sufficient for Supermarine, without the added complexity of following curving leading and trailing edges; and the move to metal wings with the S6s was, again, perhaps enough to be going on with in the limited time available before the competition. Additionally, the wire bracing reintroduced with these later aircraft made the strength/weight advantages of a more complex wing shape less obvious. It is, however, interesting to note that their uncomplicated and unbraced cantilever tailplanes were perfectly elliptical in shape.

The overseas aircraft mentioned above featured symmetrical ellipses, particularly with reference to structural considerations. Other, somewhat elliptical, wing shapes closer to home, where speed was a foremost consideration, were familiar to the Supermarine design team. Both the Short Crusader of 1927 and the Gloster VI of 1929 employed shapes which approached the elliptical, but for the narrower chord close to the fuselage – where control surfaces were not involved.

However, in the present context, the most intriguing shape was that of the Italian Piaggio P.7. While it never progressed beyond its taxiing stage, the general arrangement of this rival Italian Schneider design would surely have been known to Mitchell, and the elliptical wing shape modified by a straighter leading edge is very similar to that which was developed for the Spitfire (see drawings pp.152–3).

Also, a return to Heinkel aircraft is especially called for – in respect of the He.112 which was, in effect, a scaled-down version of the He.70 mentioned

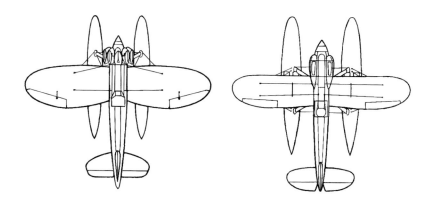

The Short Crusader.   The Gloster VI.

earlier and a contender for the contract which produced the Messerschmitt Bf.109. This latter was chosen for the Luftwaffe in October 1936 as it was smaller, lighter, and therefore offered a better performance, at the particular point in time when a decision had to be made – when it became known that the Spitfire had been ordered into production. The much improved He.112B appeared in July of the following year but did not go into service with the Luftwaffe; as its wing shape is very similar to that of the Spitfire, one wonders how formidable a fighter it might have been developed into.

The present concern, however, is to note that while some German designers were coming to similar conclusions as Mitchell, his design predated that of this rival aircraft, having been arrived at as a solution to various requirements – for both the engine weight reasons and for the aerodynamic reasons mentioned above. And it equally suited the decision to now employ a retractable undercarriage. The necessary arrangements for its housing meant that, if the machine guns were to be sited in the wing, they would have to be placed well outboard. In this respect, an elliptical form of wing was also attractive as it tapers towards the tip very slowly at first.

While the F.7/34 agreement that Mitchell was working with referred to a four-gun 'experimental' fighter, the Air Ministry requirement F.10/35 had now been issued and it repeated an earlier F.5/34 call for at least six, and preferably eight, guns to 'produce the maximum hitting power possible in the short time available for one attack'. One suspects that Supermarine and Vickers were looking well beyond their four-gun model and towards the F.5/34 requirement when the elliptical wing shape was finally decided upon. When Squadron Leader Ralph Sorley, in charge of the Operational Requirements

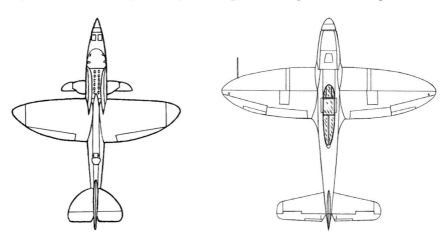

The Piaggio P.7.   The Heinkel He.112B.

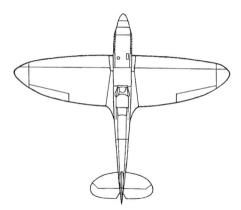

Spitfire.

section, asked if Mitchell could include four additional guns without trouble or delay, he received straightaway a quite positive response. Also, the elliptical wing, which allowed for the extra armament to be sited even further outboard, permitted their ammunition containers to be so positioned that, when emptied in action, they would not adversely alter the trim of the aircraft.

Mitchell's modified elliptical design would, theoretically, have required the optimum main spar position to curve or at least slope backwards – as projected in the Supermarine No. 300000 drawings shown earlier. However, such an arrangement would have consequent constructional and weight/strength problems and so Mitchell typically selected a less complex arrangement whereby the main spar was set at right angles to the fuselage centre line. This structural consideration had the advantage of making it easier to align the wing ribs which were to be set at progressively decreasing angles of incidence as they approached the wing tips. It also was able to follow more closely the straighter wing leading edge mentioned earlier.

The Thin Wing

The first flights of the company's Stranraer in 1934, with its thinner aerofoil, now clearly supported the developing view that the way forward for monoplanes was not represented by the thick, relatively lightly loaded wing of the Type 224 prototype. Ernest Mansbridge told Price that:

Choosing the thick section wing was a mistake when we could have used a modified, thinner section as used on the S5 floatplane … We were still very concerned about possible flutter, having encountered that with the S4 seaplane. With the S5 and S6 we had braced wings, which made things easier. But the Type 224 was to be an unbraced monoplane, and there were not many of these about at the time.

To a designer, considering the design of a wing much thinner than usual, the value of an elliptical shape was already appreciated, permitting, as it did, lightness with strength; but this concern was in order to support Mitchell's pre-established aerodynamic concerns. As C.G. Grey had noted:

> An interesting point about those Curtiss biplane racers [of 1923–1926] was that the wings came almost to a knife-edge in front [producing an extremely low thickness/chord ratio of 6 per cent]. One of the American technical people told me at the time that they had come to the conclusion that, at the speed which these machines reached, the air was compressed so much in the front of the leading edge that it paid to cut it. I passed the information on to R.J. Mitchell of Supermarine's who went into the idea quite deeply, and though he could not quite put a cutting edge on his Schneider Trophy monoplanes of 1927–1929 and 1931, he used the thinnest possible wings, and won every time.

Harry Griffiths put the matter thus:

> He had one strong fetish, namely that for maximum performance the frontal area of an aircraft had to be as small as possible, hence … his insistence on the thin wing on the Spitfire against the advice of the experts at Farnborough.

In this connection, Clifton's later comments on Mitchell's doubts about information derived from model testing deserve recording:

> I think that Mitchell decided to make the wing as thin as he did, and I wouldn't like to be positive about this, but my recollection was that it was against some advice from the National Physical Laboratory in that case where wind tunnel tests, I believe, showed that there was no advantage in going below a thickness chord ratio of 15 per cent, whereas, the [Spitfire] wing was 13 per cent at the root and 6 per cent at the tip. I believe that this was due to the fact that at that time the question of the transition from laminar to turbulent flow in relation to the difference between model and full scale wasn't understood and subsequently it was found that when you made proper allowance for that, there was an advantage, as the testing could be shown to prove, in going thinner.

At about that time, Hawkers had been advised by the National Physical Laboratory that their new wind tunnel results had shown no drag penalty with the thicker Hurricane wing. However, the laboratory scientists later found this advice to be incorrect – they attributed their earlier views to high wind tunnel turbulence, not appreciated at that time.

It is known that, by the early 1930s, Mitchell had felt that wind tunnel tests with small models might not be very helpful and so one suspects that aesthetics and intuition had quite a lot to do with the final choice of the Spitfire wing shape. (One notes that Mitchell's tail surfaces produced a more aesthetically pleasing general arrangement than those of the He.112B illustrated above.) Joe Smith was surely referring mainly to such considerations when he recorded the following description of Mitchell at the drawing board:

> He was an inveterate drawer on drawings, particularly general arrangements. He would modify the lines of an aircraft with the softest pencil he could find, and then re-modify over the top with progressively thicker lines, until one would be faced with a new outline of lines about three sixteenths of an inch thick. But the results were always worthwhile, and the centre of the line was usually accepted when the thing was redrawn.

By way of a rejoinder, one is reminded of Mitchell's forthright comment to Shenstone about the Spitfire wing: 'I don't give a bugger whether it's elliptical or not, so long as it covers the guns.' The designer is clearly acknowledging that various design compromises must shape the final outcome of a project, but one suspects he was also playing down his aesthetic concerns – Shenstone did say that the disclaimer was made 'jokingly'.

So far, little mention has been made of the input of Beverley Shenstone, who joined Supermarine at the end of 1931 and who soon became Mitchell's chief aerodynamicist. Very substantial (and, it would appear, largely unsupported) claims have been made in a recent book for his influence upon the shape of the Spitfire wing – particularly the straight leading-edge component, the shape of the trailing edge and the aerofoil selection.

One must certainly expect that the advice of this brilliant young man would not have been ignored. In Chapter 1 it has been reported how Mitchell used to call in the leaders of relevant sections and get them arguing among themselves. He would listen carefully, making sure that everyone had said what he wanted to, and then either make a decision or go home and sleep on it. Joe Smith has also indicated that he considered this quality contributed to Mitchell's leadership: 'In spite of being the unquestioned leader, he was always ready to listen to and to consider another point of view, or to modify his ideas to meet any technical criticism which he thought justified …'

One might speculate that Mitchell felt confident to pursue the very thin wing, against the technical advice mentioned above, having been supported by detailed and persuasive theoretical submissions from Shenstone. And the very final shape of the Spitfire wing might also owe a great deal to the younger man's views, as he had had direct experience of German aerodynamic theory that was well in advance of contemporary British practice. It would fit with Mitchell's habitual management style that he soon recognised that the new man might well help Supermarine to progress beyond their already acknowledged lead in high speed design. We should give the chief designer credit for not being so flushed by his earlier Schneider Trophy successes that he did not appreciate what the younger man might contribute.

On the other hand, it has been shown that Mitchell had been considering elliptical or thinner wings since the middle 1920s, and that gun and undercarriage housing (as well as aerodynamic arguments) would have been important considerations for the whole design team. Thus, recently reported diary entries by Shenstone about this period in his career are interesting:

> The elliptical wing was decided upon quite early on … The ellipse was simply the shape that allowed us the thinnest wing with sufficient room inside to carry the necessary structure and the things we wanted to cram in … Joe Smith, in charge of structural design, deserves credit for producing a wing that was both strong enough and stiff enough within the severe volumetric constraints.

It is noteworthy that the chief aerodynamicist is generous in his praise of Smith's structural input and perhaps he is too self-effacing about the importance of his own contributions, speaking impersonally about 'our' purposes and what 'we' wanted to achieve. Forty years later, at the Mitchell Memorial Symposium in Southampton, Shenstone again makes no special claims for his own input:

> I don't think R.J. cared at all what the Germans were doing but he did care about the shape of wings, but he didn't copy anything. I think all of us at the time realised that the thinnest wing can often be the best, whereas earlier, people were afraid of very thin wings in case they broke off. I think the essential thing is that Mitchell took advantage of everything he could which would improve his aircraft. Certainly Mitchell always did the thing which should be done.

At the same symposium, Clifton said, 'Meanwhile Mitchell was moving on to … a very thin wing against expert advice … Mitchell was trying to put the thing together to get the maximum possible result.' Shenstone was in the audience and one might have expected some gracious reference to the importance which has recently been claimed for him, but none is recorded. Also, in the published account of the meeting, C.F. Andrews submitted a letter he had received from Shenstone in which the latter emphasised their volumetric considerations:

> I do not think that the He.70 had much direct influence on [the] Spitfire's elliptical wing. Various wing plan forms were sketched for [the] Spitfire, and the real down to earth reason for the elliptical wing was the fact that the elliptical taper is gradual near the fuselage and can be less than that for a straight taper wing, thus giving more space for retracted undercart, and in this case also for guns.
>
> I remember that I pointed out to Mitchell that the elliptical wing was optimum for induced drag, but he said he didn't care whether it was elliptical or not as long as it had room for guns and undercart ... the real advantage of the elliptical wing turned out to be its low induced drag at very high altitudes, such altitudes not having been considered during the design, but realised during the war ... [See PR19, p.189. This last comment would seem to support the view that Mitchell was at least influenced by the aesthetics of the elliptical shape.]
>
> I think that Mitchell was fed up with wind tunnel tests after the F.7/30 [Type 224] disappointment. The only wind tunnel tests done on the Spitfire prototype were on a fairly large half model (sliced vertically stem to stern) for the sole purpose of studying the air flow through the underwing radiator.

It remains a matter of conjecture as to what interpretation one should put on Shenstone's statement that he 'pointed out' the advantage of the elliptical wing and the thin wing, or how far Mitchell had already made up his mind on these matters. Will we ever know exactly how the two minds met on this issue? We have seen that Mitchell had appreciated the value of the elliptical wing and of the thin wing before Shenstone joined Supermarine, but at least we can surely accept that Shenstone supplied detailed aerodynamic calculations which Mitchell took careful note of, and it may be that credit should be given to Shenstone for not trying to deservedly share the limelight with his famous chief designer.

Beyond that, as we have seen, the Mitchell Symposium discussion does raise questions about the precise influence of Shenstone on the complex of considerations which led to the eventual shape of the Spitfire (its importance as a document in the Mitchell story seems hardly to have been noticed elsewhere). Perhaps one can do no better than quote from a Southampton Royal Aeronautical Society (RAeS) member's summing up at this symposium:

During the discussion, Mr Clifton was asked the origin of the elliptical wing form. No authoritative reason was put forward. I am inclined to think that it was the logical result of integrating aerodynamic and structural requirements. Comparing the F.7/30 development with the Spitfire, changes are evident which must have been consciously made during the project stage.

The main spar, previously swept back, was set normal to the fuselage axis. The span, wing area and thickness to chord ratio were reduced. The straight tapered wing gave place to the elliptical form of lower aspect ratio. Thus the greater and more constant chord in the inner regions of the wing gave more space for the landing flap, undercarriage, radiator and gun installation, and provided sufficient thickness for a good structure.

For optimum bending strength the spar should have been placed at 30 per cent chord but, as this would have encroached on installation space, the 25 per cent chord position was a better choice. This must have been intentional as it was also the aerodynamic datum for the varying incidence which was progressively reduced from root to tip. From the unswept spar at 25 per cent chord the familiar asymmetric ellipse naturally followed.

The choice of a common aerodynamic and structural datum simplified work in the drawing office and hence manufacture. The unswept spar with the ribs at right angles was aerodynamically and structurally good, and simplified manufacture. The simple basic structure was the first step to low structural weight, for otherwise all the refined detail design would have been less effective …

Considering these points as a whole, and remembering the lack of precise aerodynamic date in those days, so many imponderables could only have been resolved by R.J. Mitchell's intuitive judgement; as wind tunnel work was limited to tests on spinning and the ducted radiator. As I see it, the elliptical wing is to the Spitfire as the ogee wing is to Concorde. They look right – and are right.

NAMING THE SPITFIRE

When did R.J. Mitchell say that 'Spitfire' was 'a bloody silly name' for his fighter? Dr Alfred Price noted, via the logbook of test pilot George Pickering, that the earlier Type 224 was known as the Spitfire some time before July 1935 and so Mitchell's remark might have been made about this time or earlier – when this fighter was so designated in a brief announcement by Supermarine in 1934:

The 'Spitfire' is a single-seat day and night fighter monoplane built to the Air Ministry specification. It is a low-wing cantilever monoplane with the inner sections sloping down to the undercarriage enclosures. It has a Rolls-Royce 'Goshawk' steam-cooled engine with condensers built into the wing surfaces. Armament consists of four machine guns. No further details are available for publication.

Thereafter, the revised project, following the disappointment of Type 224, was usually referred to in the works as 'the fighter' – after all, his most beautiful racer was only ever known as the 'S4'. Gordon Mitchell's book copies a Supermarine document of 29 February 1936 in which the soon-to-fly aircraft was referred to merely as the 'Modified Single-seater Fighter K5054' and he also noted that his father, 'on occasions, erroneously referred in his diary to his machine as F.37/35'. (A significant confusion between Spec F.37/34 and the later F.10/35 requirement for an eight-gun machine? – see Sorley on p.152.)

When the new design was officially named 'Spitfire' at the end of April 1936, it is just as possible that this was the time when Mitchell made the well-known comment – perhaps he did not want reminding of the disappointment of the first Spitfire or, with two years having elapsed, the original naming had faded from his mind, which was now looking towards the success of the new 'fighter'. In 1936, Supermarine publicity reads:

THE SUPERMARINE 'SPITFIRE I'
The 'Spitfire' is a single-seat day and night fighter monoplane in which much of the pioneer work done by the Supermarine Company in the design and construction of high speed seaplanes for the Schneider Trophy contests has been incorporated. [The company is silent about Type 224.] The latest technique developed by the company in flush riveted stressed-skin construction has been used, giving exceptional cleanliness and stiffness to wings and fuselage for a structure weight never before attained in this class of aircraft. The 'Spitfire' is fitted with a Rolls-Royce 'Merlin' engine, retractable undercarriage and split trailing edge flaps. It is claimed to be the fastest military aeroplane in the world.

No further details of the machine are available for publication.

It is interesting to note how, for the very first time when announcing an entirely new Supermarine design, the aircraft had been designated a Mark I. It might be that the company was merely wanting to avoid any further references to Type 224, and thus to draw a line under this less than successful machine but, in view of the many variants to be produced in the next nine years, one likes to think that the designation was prophetic.

As well as the comment, 'It's the sort of bloody silly name they would give it', Mitchell was also reported as saying that it could be called 'Spit-Blood' for all he cared. Mansbridge's daughter has recorded that 'Shrew', 'Shrike' and even 'Scarab' had also been considered, and it is a matter of speculation as to whether our chief designer would have preferred any of these. But, by this time, the Aircraft Nomenclature Committee was no more and names were now selected, in discussion with the manufacturer, by the Air Member for Supply. Vickers' suggested name for the new fighter, and accepted by the Air Ministry, was in all probability inspired by Ann McLean, the chairman's daughter, who had habitually been referred to as 'a right Spitfire'. For fighters, especially, words indicating speed and aggression were now being chosen (for example, 'Fury', 'Gladiator', 'Gauntlet, 'Whirlwind' and 'Hurricane') and 'Spitfire' more or less fell into this general category.

However, the Supermarine name also had a British pedigree. It had been applied in previous times to cannons emitting fire, to angry cats, and to anyone displaying irascibility or a hot temper, especially women – as evidenced in 1762 when Lord Amherst is quoted as saying to his mistress, 'Not so fast, I beg of you, my dear little spitfire'; and Shakespeare echoed the general sentiment when King Lear defies the elements: 'Rumble thy bellyful! Spit, fire! Spout, rain!'

In 1778, a Royal Navy vessel was named *Spitfire* – a euphemistic version of *Cacafuego*, a Spanish treasure galleon captured by Sir Francis Drake; thereafter, the navy used the name nine other times up to 1912. It was also used in the titles of several pre-war films and thus at that time was not just a relatively obscure part of the English vocabulary. By now, the word would probably have become obsolete – had it not been for the Battle of Britain and many more wartime actions involving Mitchell's fighter.

8

AFTER MITCHELL

MITCHELL'S BOMBER AND HIS DEATH

By the early part of 1937, Mitchell was to be seen less and less at Supermarine as it had now become clear that the cancer operation of 1933 had not been a successful procedure. Yet, in the last full year of his life and, even when he was still supervising the Spitfire design, another major innovative project for a bomber had been occupying his mind.

This was in response to Air Ministry specification B.12/36, which called for a high speed, four-engined bomber with a range of 3,000 miles, capable of carrying a 14,000lb bomb load or twenty-four soldiers. It also had to be able to be broken down into component parts for transport on the existing railway system and to lift off from a 500ft runway, clearing a height of 50ft at the end. For this last purpose there was the added requirement to provide a catapult take-off capability because of the small airfields currently in use and, particularly, in order to extend the bomber's potential range and load capacity.

At the same time, the wingspan was to be limited to no more than 100ft (in view of the transport considerations, rather than because of the size of existing hangars, as is often claimed). It also had to have a retractable ventral turret as well as nose and tail guns and had to be capable of staying afloat for several hours in the event of being forced down in the North Sea or Channel, as might be expected if the international situation did not improve.

ABOVE: Author's painting, based upon Supermarine drawing No. 31600, sheet 2, and Supermarine works model.

PREVIOUS: Spitfire Mark Is of No. 19 Squadron (first to be equipped with the aircraft) and the realised bomber project. (From paintings by the author)

It is interesting that Shorts and Supermarine were each awarded contracts for two prototypes rather than, for example, the Handley Page or Vickers firms which had extensive experience of the larger sort of land-based machines. But, in view of some of the Ministry requirements, it might be noted that both Supermarine and Shorts had a great deal of experience of water-resistant hulls and Supermarine had just provided the RAF and navy with the very efficient Stranraer and the catapult-stressed Walrus.

In the same month that the very positive Martlesham Heath report on K5054, the Spitfire prototype, had been received, Mitchell's tender for the bomber was sent to the Air Ministry and must have confirmed the officials' regard for Mitchell's standing in the aviation industry. Despite having a proposed wing-span of 97ft, the aircraft was to make use of a single spar wing supported by torsion-resistant leading-edge boxes on a similar principle to that developed for the much smaller Spitfire. Also, unusually for its time, fuel was to be carried in these leading edges, thereby saving weight, and with the tanks adding to the rigidity of the wing. Behind this spar component, the structure allowed sufficient room for the main stowage of bombs, thus avoiding the need for conventional tiered fuselage stowage which would have substantially increased the fuselage cross section, with the attendant penalty of extra drag.

Prior to this design, the Polish PZL P37 medium bomber had made extensive use of bomb bays in the wing between the engines and the fuselage, but Mitchell's bomb stowage arrangements in the wings was more extensive and not adopted in any of the other front-line bombers of the Second World War. Indeed, it anticipated

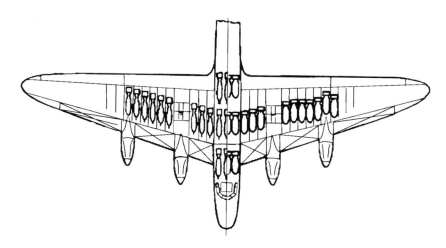

From Supermarine drawing No. 31600, sheets 5/6, showing leading edge tanks and alternative stowage of bombs: 27 × 500lb (left) and 29 × 250lb (right).

post-war designs and was further evidence of Supermarine's Schneider Trophy concerns to increase airframe efficiency by paying, instinctively as it were, particular attention to the reduction of frontal area. As a result, when Bomber Command officers inspected the Supermarine mock-up in October 1937 after Mitchell's death, they were concerned about the restricted headroom throughout the fuselage; but such were the exigencies of war, and besides, Mitchell had always made reduction of frontal area one of his first priorities.

A further refinement was the proposal to place the required armament well below the eye-line of the gunners, not only giving them an improved view but also enabling a reduction in the cross section of the turret and a more rapid traverse of the guns.

Three versions of the bomber were proposed:

1   Type 316 with Bristol Hercules engines, deltoid shaped wing and single fin (see drawing p.163 and below).
2   Type 318 with Rolls-Royce Merlin engines, but otherwise similar to 316.
3   Type 317 with Bristol Hercules engines, twin fins, and wing leading and trailing edges tapering almost equally (see model illustrated below).

Photographs of two prototype fuselages, which were almost completed before they were destroyed by enemy action, do not show what fin and wing type was to be fitted. Twin fins are illustrated opposite, with the Type 317 wing, whose equal taper design would have been less complex to design and build – an important consideration at a time when a new and more formidable bomber was urgently needed. It might also be noted that Mitchell's aerodynamicist, Beverley Shenstone, who was familiar with advanced wing theory and who was, no doubt, a strong influence on the Type 316 and 318 deltoid wing shape, left the company in 1938, and so perhaps the more conventional and less complex wing shape would most likely have prevailed.

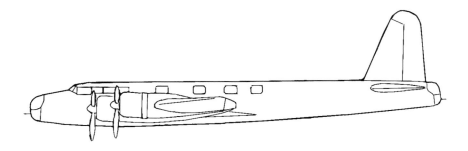

From Supermarine drawing No. 31600, sheet 1.

A Supermarine model of the Type 317 heavy bomber. (Courtesy of Solent Sky Museum)

In November 1938, Mitchell's team was able to submit a lighter and smaller design than their rival for the same specification and produced a set of estimated performance figures which make an intriguing comparison with published figures for the earliest marks of the most well-known British four-engined bombers of comparable size:

Aircraft	Power Rating	Range	Bomb Load	Max. Speed
Supermarine (est.)	1330hp	43,680 miles	8,000lb	330mph
Stirling I	1590hp	41,930 miles	5,000lb	260mph
Halifax BI	1145hp	41,860 miles	5,800lb	265mph
Lancaster I	1390hp	42,530 miles	7,000lb	287mph

More often than not, Supermarine estimates were actually achieved when their designs flew (one remembers the Spitfire performance when the right propeller was found), and so it will always be a matter of conjecture as to whether the extraordinarily competitive figures for Supermarine's proposed bomber would have been attained – and at what saving of life when war did begin. After all, it was conceived at the same time as the Stirling and Halifax, but with an estimated speed close to that of the new fighters and its projected range and bomb load were also impressive.

It might, however, be maintained that, with the need for volume production – using standard gun turrets and probably being forced to add a dorsal one too – the Supermarine estimates might have been proven to be rather optimistic in respect of a production machine.

Unfortunately, the matter remains one of rueful speculation as previous lack of urgency in aircraft development resulted in the project only reaching the stage of two prototype fuselages before they were destroyed by enemy bombing.

The chief designer never lived to learn of the fate of his last projects, just as he never actually saw his Spitfire go into squadron service before the Second World War started. Towards the end of February 1937, he went into a London hospital. The prognosis was not good and a stay at the Cancer Clinic in Vienna was arranged in the April of that year. Letters testify to his dismay at not being able to continue his input into the design of the bomber, but it had become clear that this was not possible. Mitchell returned to Southampton on 25 May 1937, the very day that his first Spitfire, Type 224, was finally retired to become a ground target at the gunnery range at Orfordness. He died on 11 June, aged 42.

As he invariably gave full credit to his design staff in his speeches, it was fitting that he requested they be given first place at his funeral, and it is perhaps significant that Harry Griffiths' recollection of Mitchell's death prompts a memory of his relationship with this team:

> On the day he died Arthur [Black, chief metallurgist] and I were standing at the bench discussing a problem when Vera Cross, R.J.'s faithful secretary over many years, came in and just said, 'It's all over'. Arthur looked at me and shook his head then he turned away and was silent for a long time.
>
> At the annual dinner that year we stood in silence in his memory and then drank a toast: 'To a very gallant gentleman.'
>
> The Christmas before his untimely death he arrived late for the annual design staff dinner, and in spite of a place having been kept for him at the head of the table he insisted on sitting at the other end with us lads and sharing a joke and some wine.

THE SPITFIRE AFTER MITCHELL

Before his death, Mitchell had had the satisfaction of attending the Vickers Press Day, where his Scapa, Walrus, Spitfire and Stranraer were all on display together. With the last three, he had produced respectively the slowest and the fastest aircraft in the RAF and the fastest biplane flying boat. Following the orders for the fifteen production Scapas and seventeen Stranraers, he then saw his company receive the orders for a total of 217 Walruses and 310 Spitfires. Here was a fitting epitaph for a designer, but he could not have imagined the extent of the future wartime requirements and varied duties of these last two aircraft, particularly the Spitfire.

Soon after the death of Mitchell, Joe Smith moved from the post of chief draughtsman to that of chief designer and the credit for fully realising the potential of Mitchell's fighter design must go to him and his team.

Joe Smith. (Courtesy of Solent Sky Museum)

Nearly thirty main variants of the Spitfire, as well as numerous modifications, followed from Mitchell's prototype, and it is a measure of the contribution of Smith and the design team to the war effort that an average of over four distinct marks of Spitfire per year were developed.

Whether Mitchell would have pursued a similar course with these modifications, or if he would have pressed the Air Ministry for a completely new design must always remain a matter of speculation. Certainly the pressures of war would not encourage the tooling-up necessary for a new type as long as modifications of existing aircraft could conceivably meet the changing wartime requirements. As Smith said, justifying his continuous modifications to the Spitfire Type, 'the hard school of war leaves no room for sentimental attachments and the efficiency of the machine as a fighter weapon is the only criterion'.

Shortly after the Hurricane entered service, Hawker had had to begin work on a new design because their current fighter did not have the potential for further development – producing the Tornado, which eventually emerged as the Typhoon and the Tempest. Joe Smith, on the other hand, had faith in the development potential of Mitchell's design, saying that it would 'see us through the war'. His Schneider Trophy experience of developing the 900hp S5 into the similar, slightly larger, 1,900hp S6 and then into the strengthened 2,350hp S6B must surely have pointed the way.

Quill identifies one other particular event that might very well have been of considerable influence upon Smith's faith in the long-term potential of

Mitchell's design – Supermarine's planned attempt on the World Land Speed record then held by the Howard Hughes' H-I racer. Compared with the current Mark I aircraft's 367mph (with a Merlin II rated at 990hp), a specially prepared Spitfire airframe and a specially rated Merlin engine (developing 2,000hp) was estimated to achieve a top speed of 425mph at sea level.

However, the venture was abandoned after Germany increased the record to 463mph. Nevertheless, Quill is surely correct that the attempt must have had a definite influence on Smith's thinking, and J.D. Scott wrote in his history of Vickers, 'By 1940 Joe Smith ... had reached the conclusion that the Spitfire design was capable of the most extensive, and indeed of almost infinite, development.' The various marks of Spitfire demonstrated that this was the case, to the extent that Rolls-Royce, when designing the Griffon engine to succeed the Merlin, tailored the new engine to fit the existing fighter's airframe.

Joe Smith's persistence with Spitfire modifications was vital to the war effort, not only because of problems with the initial Hurricane replacement, the Typhoon, but also because deliveries of the formidable Tempest only began in October 1943. Even then, the latter's top speed was not better than the Spitfire Mark XIV, which could achieve 447mph thanks to the newly employed Griffon engine.

Of course, there were economies of type development – a new mark of an existing aircraft, however radical, required much less time and effort to design than a brand new type. Woolston quotes Vickers' figures, which revealed that no later mark required more man-hours spent on design than on the Spitfire Mark I. The highest number was 165,000 man-hours devoted to the Spitfire 21, compared with 330,000 man-hours on the far less complex Mark I – with the average time per mark being about 41,000 hours.

In terms of performance figures, the extent of the developments achieved by Joe Smith and his team can be summarised by the following comparison between the first and the last production versions:

	Spitfire Mark I	Seafire 47
Maximum speed	362mph	452mph
Engine power	1050hp	2350hp
Fuel capacity	85gal	287gal (inc. 90gal drop tank)
Normal loaded weight	5820lb	10,300lb
Wing loading	24lb/sq. ft	42.2lb/sq. ft
Service ceiling	31,500ft	43,100ft
Maximum range	575 miles	1,475 miles
Climb to 20,000ft	9.4 min	4.8 min
Rate of roll at 400mph	14 degrees/sec.	68 degrees/sec.
Maximum diving speed	450mph	500mph

In the course of this development, the weight of ammunition carried had almost doubled, and that of the protective armour now amounted to more than the weight of an average pilot. Indeed, Jeffrey Quill has calculated that, at its maximum gross take-off weight, the Seafire 47 was equivalent to a Mark I Spitfire with the additional load of thirty-two 'airline standard' passengers each with 40lb of baggage.

While the extraordinary development of Mitchell's 'basic' fighter is well illustrated by the above, it would not be realistic to give too triumphal an account of the Spitfire's development. Many modifications were rather desperate attempts to avoid the production of a completely new type. Jeffrey Quill, who had by far the most extensive experience of testing the various Spitfire types, has written that almost every design change, with the urgency of wartime demands, produced problems with flight handling.

The first production Mark I, Eastleigh, May 1938. (Courtesy of E.B. Morgan)

A well-laden Seafire 47, c. 1949. (Courtesy of E.B. Morgan)

Some of the factors which most affected controllability were the progressive increase in speed and weight, in propeller blade area ('propeller solidity'), and in moments of inertia due to the redistribution of increasing weights, usually in terms of longitudinal or directional stability. Solutions were often inelegant even though usually effective.

There was also the major problem of converting the Spitfire into the Seafire for aircraft carrier operation, as the comparatively fragile land fighter had hardly been designed for the rigours of the 'controlled accidents' of landing on the pitching decks of aircraft carriers. And one particular photographic reconnaissance conversion also had its problems: the PRD/Mark IV version was found to be incapable of flying straight and level for the first half hour after take-off because of the necessary disposition of its very heavy fuel load.

But, to end on a more positive note, most photo-reconnaissance versions of the Spitfire were far less problematical, and many versions of the fighter were regarded as exceptional aircraft. In particular, perhaps the best fighter, from a handling point of view, was the Mark VIII; the most successful high-altitude fighter was the Mark XIV; the most outstanding PR (photo-reconnaissance) variant, the PR19; and the most complete naval version, the Seafire 47.

A detailed account of the twenty-seven main versions which went into quantity production is provided in Appendix 2 and indicates just how far Mitchell's basic design was capable of development, thanks to the dedicated wartime effort of Joe Smith and his design team. Meanwhile, drawings of their basic modifications will give an indication of these efforts.

The drawing opposite shows first, Mitchell's original semi-elliptical planform, followed by the clipped wing version for higher manoeuvrability at low level. The next illustration gives Smith's most obvious departure from Mitchell's original concept, the pointed wing version of the high-altitude Marks VI, VII, VIII and 21; finally, the fourth drawing shows the revised wing and tail surfaces, as seen in Marks 22 and 24.

Perhaps a more graphic illustration of the continuous development of the wartime Spitfire can be seen in its changing side views, shown on page 172. Mitchell's original design concept remained most clearly evident in the Merlin-engined fighter Mark I–II–V–IX line of development, in the PR Mark I–VII sequence and in the Seafire Mark I–II–III–XV series. The Griffon engine and the extra oil requirement in the longer range PR variants produced somewhat changed nose shapes, and increases in power also necessitated redesigns of the tail surfaces. The more powerful later Merlins had given rise to the simple change of a pointed and broader chord rudder, while the even more powerful Griffons produced a complete redesign of the unit. Another factor affecting a more fundamental redesign by other hands was the later availability of the

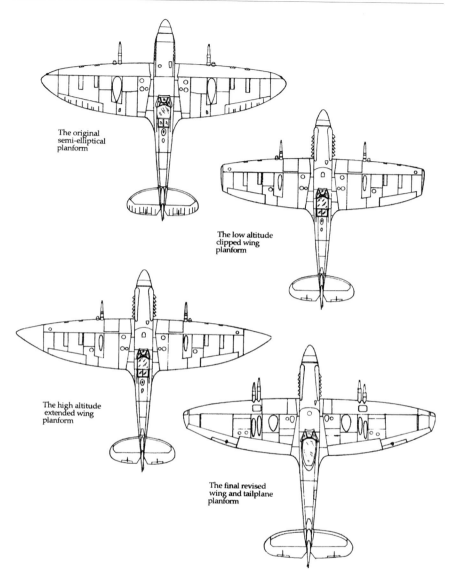

The original
semi-elliptical
planform

The low altitude
clipped wing
planform

The high altitude
extended wing
planform

The final revised
wing and tailplane
planform

Four distinctive planforms.

teardrop canopy, which resulted in a cut down rear fuselage decking and a great improvement in rear view for the pilot.

The p.169 comparison between the Mark I and the Seafire 47 gave further proof of how far Mitchell's original concept had been capable of development but, setting aside the huge difference in load carrying between the two aircraft, it can be calculated that the latter's 125 per cent increase in engine power had only produced a 25 per cent increase in speed. Thus, Mitchell's propeller design could be seen to be reaching the limits of its potential. Nevertheless, one can surely agree with Rendall's assessment of the Spitfire, that few aircraft straddled the transition between the two ages of aviation so comprehensively, let alone so elegantly – the biplane and the monoplane ages, the piston age and the jet age, the subsonic and the supersonic.

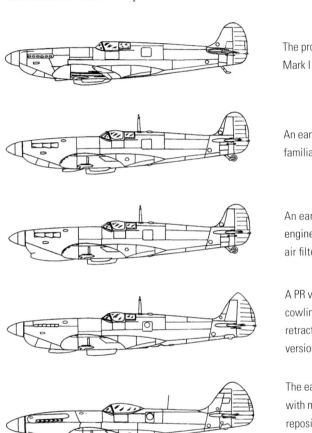

The prototype and early Mark I with flat cockpit cover.

An early mark with the more familiar domed cockpit cover.

An early mark with the 'beard' engine cowling for the tropical air filter.

A PR version with deeper engine cowling, symmetrical radiators, retractable tailwheel, and second version fin and rudder.

The early Griffon-engined type with modified engine cowling, repositioned air intake, and third version fin and rudder.

The final fighter version with balloon cockpit hood and lower rear fuselage decking, deeper radiators, and fourth version fin and rudder.

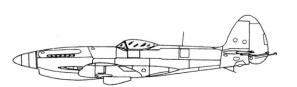

The final Seafire version with contra-rotating propellers, further revised air intake position, and modified fourth rudder.

APPENDIX 1

PHOTOGRAPHS SHOWING THE DEVELOPMENT OF THE SPITFIRE

One of the first Mark IIAs from Castle Bromwich. (Courtesy of E.B. Morgan)

The Mark V, two cannon version, with clipped wings. (Courtesy of E.B. Morgan)

The first of the three Mark V float conversions with early type tropical air filter. (Courtesy of E.B. Morgan)

A HF VII with extended wing and second version fin and rudder. (Courtesy of E.B. Morgan)

Mark XIIs of 41 Squadron. The redesigned cowling blisters for the Griffon engine are clearly evident on EB-B. (Courtesy of E.B. Morgan)

The Mark XIV, showing the five-blade right hand propeller and slightly deeper radiators. (Courtesy of E.B. Morgan)

The Mark 18, showing the camera aperture, the redesigned fin and rudder, lower fuselage decking and 'tear-drop' cockpit canopy. (Courtesy of E.B. Morgan)

The Mark F22, showing the final revisions to flying surfaces and the fourth type fin.
(Courtesy of E.B. Morgan)

Seafire F46 with contra-rotating propellers and modified fin. (Courtesy of E.B. Morgan)

APPENDIX 2

MAIN VERSIONS OF THE SPITFIRE

This book has been about Mitchell and his designs but, because of his early death, it was left to Smith and his team to fully realise the potential of his outstanding fighter. Chapter 9 has indicated the extraordinary extent of this development, but only a description of the twenty-nine main production versions can really do justice to the wartime effort that went into this continuous uprating. However, the detail of this work would seem best as an appendix as, even though it was his basic concept which had such potential, it was not Mitchell who had the oversight of it.

Mitchell's basic fighter was originally developed for high-altitude or low-altitude operation, and photo-reconnaissance work, indicated by the letters HF, LF and PR respectively (although these prefixes gradually disappeared as more versatile versions were developed). The carrier-based duties were allocated to the Seafires and there were also floatplanes and a two-seat trainer. Not all the variants went into service and, as we shall see, the mark numbers do not always indicate the actual chronology of their production.

As will also become apparent, progressive increases in performance resulted, essentially, from Supermarine's response to the remarkable supply of improved engines from Rolls-Royce, first Merlins and then Griffons.

Mark I (1,550 Built)

The Mark I was very little different in outline to Mitchell's prototype; there was, however, an increase in flap angle, and the substitution of a tailwheel for the skid. By the time of the Battle of Britain, its two-bladed propeller was replaced with a three-blade, two-position type and a slab of bulletproof glass had been attached to the outside of the front windscreen; armour plating had been fitted behind the pilot's seat and the straight-topped cockpit canopy was now dome-shaped, much to the relief of taller pilots. One particular irritant was the damage to pilots' knuckles when operating the pump to raise the undercarriage; later Mark Is had a powered system.

Control problems had also been encountered owing to the conventional practice of keeping the aileron light by using fabric covering. It was now discovered that this material tended to balloon out at speed and so the ailerons were given a metal skinning.

An investigation into the need for low drag flush riveting of all the surface panels was also undertaken by gluing split-peas over the rivet heads to simulate the standard round-headed ones and by progressively removing them from different parts of the skinning. As a result, production Spitfires had standard rivets to the fuselage while the wing surfaces continued to be flush riveted.

During the Battle of Britain, it was found that German bombers could often survive machine gun fire, thanks to their armour plating, and this led to the development of an alternative armament of two cannons and four machine guns. The Spitfires with the original eight-gun arrangement were thus designated 'IA' and the ones with the two cannons, 'IB'. Unfortunately, the cannons had to be mounted on their sides in the Spitfire's thin wing, which led to their jamming so frequently that the cannon version reverted to the eight machine gun version until the problem of stoppages could be solved.

(For PR versions of the Mark I, see the photo-reconnaissance section which follows.)

Mark II (921 Built)

The Mark II was basically similar to the later production models of the Mark I; the essential change was the fitting of the more powerful Merlin XII engine with a Rotol constant speed propeller, giving an increase in speed of 15mph and an improved climb by nearly 500ft per minute. Some were available in time to take part in the later stages of the Battle of Britain.

When the Mark II was withdrawn from front-line fighter squadrons, some were modified to operate in an air sea rescue role, by dropping dinghy and survival canisters to assist airmen until they were picked up by boat or seaplane. A small rack was also fitted to carry smoke-marking bombs. This type was redesignated 'ASR II'.

Mark III

The Mark III represented the first attempt to improve the type significantly, particularly by making the tailwheel retractable, clipping the wings and installing the Merlin XX with its two-stage supercharger. However, it was decided to give priority to upgrading the Hurricane and so the Mark III, which first flew in March 1940, never went beyond the prototype stage.

Mark IV

See the Mark XX and the photo-reconnaissance sections, below.

Mark V (6,476 Built)

The Mark V was designed as a stopgap aircraft in anticipation of a second Battle of Britain in 1941 and to counter the improved Messerschmitt Bf.109F which had greater speed and rate of climb than the Mark II. With the new Merlin 45, the Mark V now had a top speed of 376mph, an operating ceiling of 36,000ft, and was able to climb to 20,000ft in six minutes.

This mark came out in three versions, now that the cannon jamming problem had been overcome. The VA retained the original eight machine gun layout; the VB had two 20mm cannon and four machine guns; and the VC had four cannons, a repositioned undercarriage, and could carry a 500lb bomb under the fuselage – thanks to the fitting of the stronger wing of the Mark III.

As the strengthened 'C' wing also allowed for the 'A' and 'B' gun arrangement, it was known as the 'universal' wing and represented an important development, paving the way for the introduction of the ubiquitous Mark IX.

There was also a float-equipped version, originally intended to operate from fjords, in response to the German invasion of Norway, and the Japanese entry into the war gave rise to a later consideration of the type, to be based where the terrain was unsuitable for the provision of airfields. Three Mark VB machines were specially equipped with floats, fittingly designed by Arthur Shirvall, who was responsible for those of the Supermarine Schneider Trophy winners. In view of its Schneider Trophy predecessors, it is not surprising that the test pilot found that 'it was a most beautiful floatplane and all we had to do, predictably, was to increase the fin area to compensate for the float area ahead of the centre of gravity'. Thus, underfins, unique to the floatplane Spitfire, were fitted with a later addition of a fillet to the leading edge of the dorsal fin. These aircraft were sent in the end to Alexandria but never saw operational service.

The Mark V was produced before America had joined the war and when Britain was heavily engaged in the Mediterranean and North African campaigns. It therefore appeared in larger numbers than any other Spitfire mark, remaining the main RAF fighter until the summer of 1942. The low-level (LF) Mark V continued in use into 1946.

Mark VI (100 Built)

The Mark VI signified the first serious move to improving the current ceiling of the Spitfire V. The necessary increase in wing area was achieved by the somewhat ad hoc expedient of adding pointed tips (which completely compromised the appearance of Mitchell's original conception). The fitting of a pressurised cockpit also left much to be desired, as the hood had to be locked on before take-off and could not be opened in flight; and while it could be jettisoned in an emergency, the hood had to be completely removed for normal entrance and exit.

This variant, equipped with a Merlin 47 engine and a four-blade propeller, was produced at the end of 1941, in response to the fear of Germany sending over high flying bombers, with a ceiling approaching 45,000ft. However, the German invasion of Russia caused these fears to recede and so this mark was not produced in large numbers.

Mark VII (140 Built)

The Mark VII represented, along with the Mark VIII, a significant step in the development of the Spitfire, thanks to the Merlin 61 with its two-stage, two speed supercharger. However, it was not produced immediately after Marks V and VI because substantial design changes were to be made – including the incorporation of fuel tanks in the wings, 11 gallons more fuel capacity in the fuselage and (finally) a retractable tailwheel. Also, the pressurised cockpit was now provided with a sliding hood, although with no hinged door in the side of the fuselage. The top speed was now 416mph.

It began to appear in August 1942, and later aircraft were fitted with an extended fin and broader chord rudder. The HF version, with a Merlin 71, continued the use of the expanded span wing tips. However, the Mark IX was now being produced as another stopgap measure, and because of its improved performance no large production orders were placed for the Mark VII. Many of these variants were used for meteorological work.

Mark VIII (1,658 Built)

The Mark VIII, which appeared a year later, was the fourth most numerous variant, supplied with standard, clipped or extended wings for its many duties. Extra tanks in the wing roots now increased the fuel capacity to 124 gallons and a 250lb bomb could be carried under each wing. The Mark VIII was now tropicalised, without the bulky 'beard' air filter housing that had been fitted to the Mark V and it was used extensively in the Middle East, India, Burma and Australia.

As with the Mark VII, the ailerons were modified and, with the Merlin 66 engine, resulted in an aircraft which was assessed by Jeffrey Quill: 'I always thought the aeroplane which was the best from the pure text book handling point of view was the Mark VIII … With the standard wing-tip it was a really beautiful aeroplane'.

Mark IX (5,653 Built)

The Mark IX, like the Mark V, was planned as a short-term expedient, this time in response to the Focke-Wulf 190, which began to appear over northern France in late 1941, when it was found to out-climb, out-run and out-manoeuvre the Spitfire V.

The Mark IX began to be produced in June 1942, and was essentially the earlier machine fitted with improved Merlins. The standard fighter had the Merlin 61 and 63, the low-altitude version had the Merlin 66, and the high-altitude aircraft the Merlin 70. These three versions were designated, respectively, F IX, LF IX, and HF IX.

Lightened versions could now fly higher than the specially designed Mark VI, and one Mark IX is celebrated as engaging in the highest air battle of the Second World War – stripped of armour plating and with only two cannons, it pursued a Junkers Ju 86 bomber up to 43,000ft and damaged it before its guns jammed. This action took place, fittingly, over Southampton.

The new mark's top speed had now risen to 408mph and marked the point where the dedicated record-breaking S6B was overtaken in level flight by a fully equipped fighting machine. The new Merlins now required a four-bladed propeller to absorb the increased power, and the need for increased cooling resulted in symmetrical underwing radiator ducting for the first time.

However, when the Mark IX was tested against a captured Fw.190 in July of the following year (Oberleutnant Armin Faber had conveniently landed it, a little lost, at RAF Pembrey Sands on 23 June 1942), the differences in performance were too small for comfort and the German's rate of climb between 15,000 and 23,000ft was superior.

Fortunately, Rolls-Royce were able to respond with the improved Merlin 66, and later, as with most aircraft after 1944, it was also fitted with a 'teardrop' canopy and lowered rear fuselage decking, giving it more speed and far better rearward visibility. Also, the supply of two 18 gallon fabric fuel cells in the wings and a 72 gallon tank in the rear fuselage produced an internal fuel capacity which was nearly twice that of the prototype Spitfire. With the addition of a 45 gallon drop tank, Jeffrey Quill flew a Mark IX from Salisbury Plain to the Moray Firth and back – the equivalent of East Anglia to Berlin and back – at less than 1,000ft.

While the 'C' wing, with four machine guns and two cannons, was stand-ard, an 'E' wing was introduced later and was equipped with the two cannons, together with two larger bore ½in Browning machine guns. Accordingly, two new designations were used: LF IXE and HF IXE.

(There was also another floatplane conversion, in 1944, with the modified fin of the Mark V conversion, but no production orders materialised.)

After the war, a 1941 proposal for a two-seat trainer version was revived and a Mark VIII Spitfire was converted by the expedient of moving the cockpit 13½ inches further forward, to allow for a separate instructor's cockpit that was behind and above the front one. Twenty Mark IX aircraft were thus converted and sold abroad.

The Mark IX, although intended as a stopgap type, was the second most numerous version.

Marks X and XI

See the photo-reconnaissance section, below.

Griffon-engined Spitfires

Rolls-Royce, before the outbreak of the war, had been developing a larger ver-sion of the Merlin engine, with a capacity of 36.7 litres instead of the 27 litres of its predecessor, to be known as the Griffon, and on 8 November 1939 N.E. Rowe of the Air Ministry suggested that it should be fitted to the Spitfire. Despite its much larger capacity, Rolls-Royce produced an engine which had a frontal area no more than 6 per cent greater and a length no more than 3in greater than its Merlin predecessors. Thus it became possible to adapt the Spitfire airframe to the enormously more powerful engine and to prolong the development of the Spitfire until the end of the war and after.

The first Griffon-engined prototype was originally designated Mark IV but, as other types were required before it could be fully developed, the aircraft was specified as the Mark XX. Quill has recorded that, in July 1942, he was asked to take part in a comparison test with the new Hawker Typhoon and a captured Fw190. He chose the new Griffon-engined prototype, DP845, which had first flown in the previous November and caused quite a stir: while the Fw190 had to drop back due to engine trouble, Quill was able to leave the leave the Typhoon well behind.

Mark XII (100 Built)

The Mark XII became the first production version of a Griffon-engined Spitfire. It was intended for low-level operation and used the single-stage Griffon III, with clipped wings as standard. It was based on the VC airframe, but had the newer, pointed, broad-chord fin and rudder. Some of the earlier XIIs had fixed tailwheels, but the distinguishing feature of all Griffon-engined types was the engine cowling – now modified with blisters over the cylinder banks of the new engine to leave a trough down the centre of the longer nose to assist the forward view of the pilot. With the new engine and new fin and rudder, the length of the type was now extended to 31ft 10in.

Nevertheless, the Mark XII was an improvised machine with a poor rate of climb because of its single-stage supercharged engine. It was only built in limited numbers and was phased out in September 1945. The Spitfire Mark IX was still the most useful all-round fighter.

Mark XIII

See the photo-reconnaissance section below.

Mark XIV (957 Built)

The Mark XIV was required in order to improve on the high-altitude performance of both the Mark IX and the Mark XII. This was achieved with the fitting of a Griffon 65 engine with two-stage supercharging. The new power unit now made separate high or low-altitude versions unnecessary. Indeed, with the new two-stage engine, it was very successful at low level against the German V1s and was also the main superior high-altitude fighter until the end of the war.

However, the Mark XIV was another interim type, with some directional instability, as with the previous Griffon mark, and so the required fin and rudder area eventually produced the first thorough redesign of these components. The power of the latest Griffon engine now required a five-bladed propeller and the radiators were slightly deeper.

Quill reported that it called for vigilant flying – particularly because, as part of a move towards standardisation, the Griffon engine rotated in the opposite direction from the Merlin and so the swing during take-off was not only more powerful but was now to the right. Also, only slight throttle movements resulted in a dramatic surge of power. Nevertheless, Quill's first impression of the new machine was expressed in his phrase 'quantum jump', for the performance was spectacular: 445mph at 25,000ft and a climb of over 5,000ft per minute.

The new mark was the first Spitfire in the fighter-reconnaissance (FR) category, which signified the use of standard fighters equipped with cameras and operating as fighter-reconnaissance aircraft. It could be equipped with four cannons and could carry bombs, so it could claim to have the best all-round performance of any current fighter apart from range. Later versions had the improved rear-view 'teardrop' canopy with the lower fuselage decking.

It was the last substantial production run of any type of Spitfire and the last version to see significant action. The first Mark XIVs were produced in time to take part in the invasion of Europe in June 1944, and one had the distinction of being the first aircraft to shoot down the formidable Messerschmitt Me262 jet fighter.

Many hundreds were sent to assist with the Pacific War, but this ended before many saw active service.

Mark XV

See the Seafire section below.

Mark XVI (1,053 Built)

From September 1944, a version of the Mark IX was produced, powered by the low-rated Merlin 66 built under licence by the Packard Motor Co. of Detroit. It came with the 'E' wing and the modified 'rear-view' fuselage. Clipped wings were standard as the machine was to be used mainly for ground attack. It had the separate LF XVIE designation.

Mark XVII

See the Seafire section below.

Mark 18 (300 Built)

(NB: from 1943, it became the RAF convention to use Arabic numerals, rather than the Roman numerals used for previous marks.)

The Mark 18 was very similar to the Mark XIV, also powered by the Griffon 65 (later replaced with the 67 version) and it incorporated the later aspects of the Mark XIV, including the rear-view fuselage and retractable tailwheel. The wings, however, were a redesigned unit with a strengthened centre-section and with a wider track undercarriage; fuel capacity was also increased.

As it was produced two years after the Mark XIV, it was too late for wartime service; it did, nevertheless, see action as late as 1951 against Communist forces in Malaya.

Mark 19

See the photo-reconnaissance section, below.

Mark XX

For the Mark XX (so designated because it was proposed before the use of Arabic mark numerals) see the introduction to the Griffon-engined Spitfires above.

Mark 21 (121 Built)

The Mark 21 was similar in many ways to the Mark 18, but the wings were of the extended span type. It was soon supplied with the first completely revised wing in which the familiar Mitchell outline was significantly altered – with half-rounded tips, and redesigned and larger ailerons.

RAF test pilots did not consider it an improvement on the Mark XIV as an all-round machine and advised that 'no further attempt should be made to perpetuate the Spitfire family'. On the other hand, Quill found the new mark to have 'a tremendous lightness of control' and 'revelled in aerobatics at speeds that would have been impossible before'. The major redesign work involved had been put in hand by 1942 but this mark was only operational at the end of 1944. It was not produced in large numbers because the war ended soon after its production began.

Mark 22 (268 Built)

The Mark 22 was also completed very late – in 1945 – and its development from the Mark 21 was so seamless that no prototype, as such, was necessary. The main difference between the two variants was the increased fuel capacity of the later mark.

While the Mark 21 still retained the balloon type of cockpit hood and its associated rear fuselage decking, the later machine was equipped from the outset with a final rear-view fuselage and canopy configuration. A redesigned wing and tailplane was fitted and a fourth type of fin.

Mark 23

The Mark 23 was never built.

Mark 24 (74 Built)

Given the revised wing and tail planforms and increased fuel capacity, the resultant manoeuvrability and increased range made the Mark 24 the 'ultimate Spitfire', and showed how far it had been possible to develop Mitchell's prototype of 1936. One does, however, tend to agree with Quill: 'The genius passed on by Mitchell had died. The beautiful symmetry had gone; in its place stood a powerful, almost ugly fighting machine.'

This final Spitfire came off the production line in February 1948.

Photo-Reconnaissance Spitfires

As with the naval Seafire (see below), the photo-reconnaissance version had never been envisaged by Mitchell, although the 'Speed Spitfire', a modified Mark I which failed to establish a new speed record, set the pattern for highly polished and unarmed Spitfires being developed for the reconnaissance role.

Various rather ad hoc camera placings, usually under the wings, and different fuel tankage arrangements were indicated by designations PR IB to PR IG, with the D long-range version becoming developed as the PR IV, which was the mainstay of the RAF Reconnaissance Unit until 1941, and 229 were built.

PR VI (6 Built)

The PR VI was a special conversion of Mark VI fighters sent to the Middle East in 1942 for PR work.

PR VII

See PR IG, which was used for low-level work and so retained its armour.

PR Mark X (16 Built)

The PR Mark X saw the use of the new, more powerful Merlin 61 for PR work, with the usual bulletproof windscreen deleted in favour of a plain, curved one. This, in combination with wing leading edges without gun ports, gave an increase of 5mph in speed over a standard Mark IX fighter. The Mark XI appeared before the PR Mark X as the latter had a pressurised cockpit and this involved a longer developmental period.

PR Mark XI (471 Built)

The PR Mark XI had the fuselage camera installations of the long-range PR Mark IV, later augmented by a camera fitted in a blister under each wing, just outboard of the wheel well. As this long-range mark was also fully tropicalised, it not only served in Europe but was also employed in the Middle East and the Pacific. As a result, it was the main PR variant of the Second World War and could be regarded as the most effective RAF photo-reconnaissance aircraft.

It achieved the highest wartime speed of any Spitfire when being tested at Farnborough. On 27 April 1944, Squadron Leader 'Marty' Martindale dived from 40,500ft to a speed of 606mph (Mach 0.89) before the engine blew up. He glided safely back to the airfield, despite almost no forward vision owing to a heavily oiled windscreen.

PR Mark XIII (26 Built)

The PR Mark XIII signified an advance on the PR VII low-level reconnaissance aircraft and was, essentially, a Mark V fitted with a special low-altitude rated Merlin 32 and a 30 gallon drop tank. It appeared in 1943 – by which time standard fighters were also being equipped, additionally, with cameras and operated as fighter-reconnaissance (FR) aircraft.

PR Mark 19 (225 Built)

The PR Mark 19 was the only Griffon-powered PR variant. The Griffon 65 was later replaced by the Griffon 66, and the aircraft had a pressurised cockpit, now that cruising at increased height was possible. The leading-edge fuel tanks were increased by 20 gallons on each side, giving a total internal petrol capacity of 256 gallons, often supplemented by a 90 or 170 gallon drop tank.

This airframe, which was produced in May 1944, and, with the full advantage of the Griffon engine, resulted in one of the most outstanding of all the Spitfire variants. With a top speed of 460mph, it was one of the fastest piston-engined aircraft of all time and could cruise at 370mph and at 40,000ft, beyond the reach even of the German jets at the end of the war – or, indeed, beyond the reach of any jet until the early 1950s. Flight Lieutenant E.C. Powles claimed a climb to 51,550ft and an emergency dive, when his cabin pressurisation failed, to a speed of Mach 0.96 (NB: not with a machine fitted with a later revised wing, but with the last mark to embody the classic elliptical wing of Mitchell's original design).

It was produced in time for the closing stages of the war in Europe and saw limited service in the Pacific and Far Eastern areas. In 1957, a Meteorological Flight of Mark 19s was finally phased out.

The Seafires

At the beginning of the war, naval aviation was underdeveloped – attributed, by C.G. Grey, to the senior Admirals being 'definitely anti-air-minded' and being 'solid ivory from the jaws up, except for a little hole from ear to ear to let useful knowledge go in and out'. And he attributed the sinking of the *Prince of Wales* and the *Repulse* off the coast of Malaya and the prolonged hunting of the *Bismarck*, *Scharnhorst* and *Prinz Eugen* to lack of effective naval aircraft.

The navy's first all-metal monoplanes were the relatively slow Blackburn Skua dive-bomber, and the even slower Roc. The later Fairey Fulmar was far too large and unwieldy when it came up against the new single-seat opposition now based on the other side of the Channel, and so the Admiralty had requested a navalised version of both the Spitfire and the Hurricane.

Some sixty Hurricanes were put into service as a stopgap but, by mid-1942, mounting losses made it urgent that Spitfires should be finally employed. So it came about that the first Seafires were basically Spitfire Vs fitted with arrester hooks and, because they were fitted with the B wing, were designated Seafire IB and IIB.

The Mark II was also equipped for catapult launching and, because of the harsher nature of seaborne landings, was now given a strengthened undercarriage. The designation Seafire IIC signaled the fitting of the 'universal' wing to this version, followed by FR IIC which signified the installation of cameras. This aircraft entered service in June, 1942, and its first action was in support of Albacore bombers during Operation Torch. (In total, 372 Seafires I and II were produced.)

Seafire Mark III (1,250 Built)

The Seafire Mark III (not to be confused with the Spitfire III prototype) saw the introduction of folding wings, which allowed its use on a wider variety of vessels. Because of the extensive modification required to the wings, the Mark III did not become operational until late 1943 and it was still in service at the end of the war with Japan.

Seafire Mark XV (390 Built)

The Seafire Mark XV was the first naval version to be equipped with the Griffon engine and was basically a Seafire Mark III airframe with manually operated folding wings, a Spitfire Mark VIII tail and retractable tailwheel, and on later aircraft, a newly designed spring-loaded 'sting' deck arrester hook, involving a modification to the rudder. It finally began appearing in September 1944.

Seafire Mark XVII (233 Built)

The Seafire Mark XVII was the first naval type with the later cut down fuselage and rear-view canopy, and it now had a curved windscreen and was equipped for rocket-assisted take-offs. With the previous folding wing arrangement retained, but with a strengthened main spar and long-stroke undercarriage, this mark can therefore be regarded as the first dedicated carrier-Spitfire.

It began to appear in September 1945, four years after the first improvised naval versions but too late for wartime service. However, it did gave the navy its first 400mph machine.

Seafire Mark 45 (51 Built)

The Seafire Mark 45 appeared soon after the Mark XVII, despite its much higher mark number – which had been allocated to allow for future Spitfires which were, in fact, never produced. It was 45mph faster than the previous type, but its more powerful Griffon 61 engine produced a swing on take-off which was not exactly ideal for carrier operation. Some later aircraft were fitted with contra-rotating airscrews which, together with an increase in rudder area, made a considerable improvement.

Seafire Mark 46 (25 Built)

The above modifications, with a tail destined for the future Spiteful fighter, constituted the Mark 46 although it did not have folding wings, as there had not been time to develop such an arrangement for the new type of wing of the Spitfire Mark 21 on which it was based.

Seafire Mark 47 (90 Built)

The Seafire 47 combined the improvements of Marks 45 and 46, and was also finally equipped with a powered wing-folding geometry. The air intake filter was now faired into the lower engine cowling, with the duct opening positioned just behind contra-rotating propellers. Combined with a top speed of 452mph, it can be seen as the most comprehensive naval revision of the Spitfire land plane and an impressive illustration of how far it had been possible to develop Mitchell's original conception. It saw service in the Korean War.

(N.B. On the website www.airhistory.org.uk/spitfire/home.html (accessed 24.11.14), the author admits that it will probably never be possible to give a definitive listing, 'owing to errors and omissions in official records'. Thus even his impressive record of the serial numbers and service history of every machine identified cannot guarantee the number of various makes are *entirely* accurate.)

APPENDIX 3

SUPERMARINE WOODEN HULLS

One of the fortuitous circumstances in R.J. Mitchell's career was joining a firm which had experience of a method of flying boat hull construction of considerable potential, while wooden hulls were in vogue.

It is perhaps necessary to give some detail of this technique of sophisticated marine know-how which was so important in the early career of the young chief designer from the landlocked Potteries and from a background in locomotive engineering. However, an adequate account was considered to be too detailed for inclusion in the main body of this book and so it is given here. A further reason for the inclusion of this detail is that visitors to the RAF Museum at Hendon may appreciate better this early technique, as exemplified in the splendidly restored Supermarine Southampton hull (see photograph overleaf).

As described in Chapter 1, the workforce of the Pemberton-Billing firm were largely 'Kemp boatyard men' and that his PBI hull was 'of round construction, built by small boat methods, with closely spaced wooden ribs of half inch square section like girl's hoops, joined by longitudinal stringers and covered by two layers of mahogany or cedar wood planking, laid so that the outside layer was sloping the opposite way to the inner layer'. There was a layer of doped fabric between, and the whole was fastened by brass screws or copper nails.

With the outbreak of the First World War, an Admiralty design team had joined the yacht designer, Linton Hope, at Woolston to further develop flying boat hull construction and so the basic structure with which Supermarine afterwards continued was established.

The standard reconnaissance flying boat of the First World War, derived from American models, had been the Felixstowe, but its slab-sided hull had structural and hydrodynamic deficiencies. The Air Ministry were concerned to see if the Linton Hope type of hull could be used instead on aircraft of the Felixstowe size and so, in 1917, specifications had been issued for this purpose. Captain David Nicolson, in two articles for *Flight*, described these and strongly advocated the Linton Hope approach they embodied:

> Being of circular cross section, with fair and easy lines, they offer much less air resistance, consequently with the same horsepower are driven at higher speeds; they are much stronger weight for weight than the F [Felixstowe] Type, more seaworthy, and generally show the impress of the trained naval architect's hand.

However, such hulls could not be evaluated immediately, as the manufacturers of larger seaplanes were fully committed to the wartime production of standard service machines. Supermarine and Mitchell's good fortune was that the building of two smaller prototypes employing Linton Hope methods had been contracted out to the Pemberton–Billing firm and, although Hope did

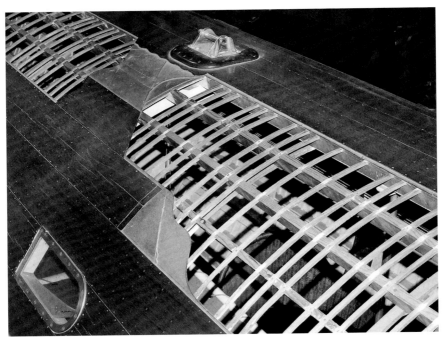

Detail of the restored Southampton hull, showing the close-spaced hoops, the lengthwise stringers and the outer skin of longitudinal thin mahogany strips, also, the rear main point for the wing attachment.

not entirely get his own way, as he indicated in another *Flight* article, the less than perfect machines embodied the alternative and much more promising approach to flying boat hull design:

> These [Pemberton-Billing] boats were very difficult to get off the water … and with later experience it was obvious that the main step was too far aft and the rear step much too far forward … In spite of these faults in design, the AD Boats showed the great strength of the flexible construction, and some bending and crushing tests carried out by the RAE works at Farnborough Show what they were able to resist.

When Mitchell became chief designer and chief engineer, he fixed on this Linton Hope structure as the standard company approach to flying boat hulls, particularly because of its shock absorption when landing on choppy water – there being no possibility of any of the conventional springing available to land planes. As C.G. Grey said of these hulls: 'They were almost basket-like in their flexibility, and so got through the water without that jarring shock which was common to most high speed motor boats.'

A small example of attention to the interface between rigidity and flexibility is mentioned in a *Flight* article about the Sea King:

> [The pilot's] controls are mounted on the triangular tubular frame so well known in all Supermarine boats, and whose function it is to allow the circular hull to flex and 'give' in a seaway, without interfering with the smooth working of the controls.

This approach and its method of construction were also spoken of approvingly in a lecture to the Royal Aeronautical Society given by Captain Nicholson, who had been involved with the alternative flat-sided hulls of the Felixstowe flying boats:

> Construction is such that the structure is capable of resilient distortion, so that when alighting it can spring, reducing the shock. The hull cross section is egg-shaped, very light, possesses great strength, and is built of longitudinal stringers with bent hoop timbers inside and light frames outside the stringers, skinned with double planking, through-fastened together. No web frames or cross-bracings are required, and the hull is a continuous structure with steps externally added.

Webb, during his apprenticeship in the hull-building section, also noted how the brass nails and screws that held the final planking in place had to be fixed precisely in line and how the hull was then finally sanded down by hand and varnished until it had a surface 'akin to the best kept dining room table'. Cozens used a similar comparison: 'All through the lifetime of the wooden flying boats the air of sturdy solidarity was due to the beautiful diagonal mahogany or red cedar planking of the hulls, covered by four coats of copal varnish, which gave it a look of a piece of well-polished furniture.'

As Webb joined Supermarine in 1926, it would appear that he was speaking of work on the later Southampton flying boats, and it is also possible that Cozen's account is influenced by the memories of the later machines' finish – readers today are now able to see the magnificently restored Southampton hull at the RAF Museum, Hendon, and confirm for themselves the carefully aligned brass fixings and the 'luxury yacht' planked finish. (The positioning of the outer layer can be seen to be laid longitudinally; the practice of placing a layer of varnished fabric between the two layers was continued with.)

Unfortunately, photographs of the earlier aircraft do not show details of planking and so it is not clear whether the final finish was always varnished wood, as described above, or a doped-on fabric, also varnished. There is also evidence that at least some of the earlier machines, which were smaller and lighter than the Southampton, were not entirely double-planked but built with a single skin of planking: Supermarine themselves gave a description of variant construction, with reference to their earlier Sea King II:

> The hull is of circular construction with built-on steps, which can be replaced in case of damage. The steps are divided into watertight compartments, the top side being of single-skin planking, covered with fabric treated with a tropical doping scheme.

Also a *Flight* description of the machine says that:

> The boat hull is of the typical Supermarine type, boat-built and through-fastened, with copper or brass fixings throughout. The mahogany single-skin planking is riveted to rock elm timbers and frames, and covered externally with fabric suitably treated with pigmented dope.

Further, the Sea Lion III is also described as having 'mahogany single-skin planking ... covered externally with fabric suitably treated with pigmented dope'. One is reminded of Cozens' report that, when the Sea Lion (Mark II, as it then was) was first started up, the vibration at the tail was so great that the pilot refused to fly it until the rear fuselage had been stiffened up – by wrapping and gluing *more* canvas around it.

It should be noted that the Sea King and the Sea Lion shared a common ancestry, and probably the same fuselage, with the earlier N1B Baby – hence the similarity in the above extracts – and so it would seem that Mitchell had inherited an aircraft whose construction had been significantly lightened in order to achieve the very sprightly performance it undoubtedly had. Specific centre of gravity considerations or design requirements might very well have led to Mitchell requiring variations in planking and finishing in other of the firm's aircraft at about this time – for example a Supermarine patent allows for planking to be omitted where external steps are to be added:

If it is desired to reduce the weight of the hull to the greatest possible extent, the skin-planking on the hull proper may be omitted where side wings or other projections cover that portion of the hull. Where this planking is omitted it is preferred to use a fabric covering for the hull proper so that it is maintained watertight, even although the wing or other projection may be perforated. The close spacing of the bent timbers and stringers provide sufficient support for the fabric to be a satisfactory watertight skin in cases of emergency.

Thus, when we consider Mitchell's first complete designs, the Commercial Amphibian, Sea Eagle, Seagull II/III, Seal II and Scarab/Sheldrake, which can be regarded as coming from a common stable, some or all may also have had canvas exteriors. Indeed, *Flight* describes the Seal II as 'boat-built of planking over a light skeleton of timbers and stringers, and covered in fabric on the outside'.

The machines in this group are, however, all about 11ft longer than the previously mentioned machines and would probably require the stiffening of double planking, especially bearing in mind the need here to design more staid, robust designs.

There is an intriguing report in *Flight* of the visit of HRH the Prince of Wales to Supermarine, where it is said that 'the building of the Seagull flying boat hulls was greatly admired by His Royal Highness'. Perhaps the company saw an advantage in producing hulls that were, prior to the Southampton, fine examples of the boat-builder's art, bearing in mind the naval backgrounds of their British, Australian and Spanish customers. But it could be that the prince merely saw well-finished planking awaiting a protective layer of fabric to be doped on.

It is also worth considering that wherever there was double planking, with the usual layer of canvas in between, fabric might also have been applied externally to protect the woodwork from splitting in the sun as well as to prevent the soaking up of water – one thinks particularly of the Scarabs for Spain or the 'tropicalised' Seagull IIIs for Australia. The commonly held view that Supermarine hulls were a mahogany colour might be accounted for either because of a varnished wood finish or because the doped-on fabric would allow the colour of the timber to show through. And, of course, the 'pigmented dope' chosen might be mahogany in hue and none too opaque, given that Supermarine might very well have been strongly attached to reminders of their boating heritage.

Thus, more than 100 years after Pemberton-Billing and then Supermarine had begun to lay down these early hulls, there is a lack of information as to the precise structure of the various aircraft and one must be careful not to generalise. But, with this proviso, it can be clearly appreciated what was the essence of the Linton Hope contribution to flying boat design which Mitchell was fortunate to inherit and whose early structural virtues he must have valued.

ACKNOWLEDGEMENTS

Putnam's book on Supermarine, and the annual publications of *Jane's* have been invaluable sources of information, as has Price's work on the genesis of the Spitfire. The reminiscences of various test pilots (notably Biard and Quill) and the RAF High Speed Flight officers (especially Orlebar and Schofield) have also provided valuable insights. Additionally, the works of Penrose, Viscount Templewood and Sinnot have been very helpful sources of information concerning the economic and political factors affecting British aircraft development during this period.

In the particular context of Supermarine, the extracts from publications by colleagues of Mitchell, especially Webb and Griffiths, have been most informative. Also, the unpublished manuscript of Cozens, helpfully copied to me by Solent Sky Museum.

Every effort has been made to gain permissions to reproduce material, but if there have been any omissions please contact the publisher who will include a credit in subsequent printings or editions. I have been unable to contact the following publishers or estates of authors: Collins (Templewood), Foulis (Nicholl), C.G. Grey, Hamilton (Schofield), Hurst & Blackett (Biard), J&KH Publishing (Webb), AFC Seeley Service and Co. (Orlebar), and United Writers (Griffiths).

The drawings and paintings are my own, as are the photographs, unless otherwise credited.

I am also appreciative of the kind assistance I have received in the past from the Royal Air Force Museum, Cambridge University Department of Manuscripts & Archives, The Royal Aeronautical Society and the staff at Southampton Solent Sky Museum, especially the director, Squadron Leader Alan Jones, whose early encouragement was much appreciated.

BIBLIOGRAPHY

'The Air Yacht', *Twenty-First Profile*, Vol. 1, No. 9.

Alcorn, J., 'Battle of Britain Top Guns', *The Aeroplane Monthly*, September 1996.

Alcorn, J., 'Battle of Britain Top Guns Update', *The Aeroplane Monthly*, July 2000.

Allen, H. Warner, *Lady Houston DBE* (Constable, 1947).

Andrews, C.F., and E.B. Morgan, *Supermarine Aircraft since 1914* (Putnam, 1981).

Andrews, C.F., and E.B. Morgan, *Vickers Aircraft since 1908* (Putnam, 1974).

'B.12/36 Bomber', *Twenty-First Profile*, Vol. 1, No. 6.

Barker, R., *The Schneider Trophy Races* (Chatto & Windus, 1971).

Barnes, C.H., *Bristol Aircraft since 1910* (Putnam, 1964).

Barnes, C.H., *Shorts Aircraft since 1900* (Putnam, 1967).

Battle, H.F.V. OBE DFC, *Line!* (Newbury, 1984).

Bazzocchi, Dr E., 'Technical Aspects of the Schneider Trophy and the World Speed Record for Seaplanes', *Journal of the Royal Aeronautical Society*, February 1972.

Biard, H.C., *Wings* (Hurst & Blackett, 1935).

Black, A., 'R.J. Mitchell – Designer of Aircraft', *The Reginald Mitchell County Primary School Commemorative Brochure*, 1959.

Buchanan, Major J.S., 'The Schneider Cup Race, 1925', Proceedings of the 10th meeting, 61st session of the Royal Aeronautical Society.

Cozens, G.A., 'Concerning the Aircraft Industry in South Hampshire'. Unpublished manuscript, Solent Sky Museum.

Day, J. Wentworth, *Lady Houston DBE* (Allan Wingate, 1958).

Doyle, N., *From Sea-Eagle to Flamingo* (The Self-Publishing Association Ltd, 1991).

Duval, G.R., *British Flying-Boats and Amphibians, 1909–1952* (Putnam, 1966).

Eves, E., *The Schneider Trophy Story* (Airlife Publishing, 2001).

'Forty Years of the Spitfire', Proceedings of the R.J. Mitchell Memorial Symposium, 6 March 1976 (Royal Aeronautical Society, Southampton Branch).

Godwin, J., 'Early Aeronautics in Staffordshire', Staffordshire Libraries, Arts & Archives, 1986.

Greig, Air Commodore D'Arcy A., *My Golden Flying Years* (Grub St, 2010).

Grey, C.J., *Sea Flyers* (Faber & Faber, 1942).

Griffiths, Harry 'Griff', *Testing Times: Memoirs of a Spitfire Boffin* (United Writers, Cornwall, 1992).

Hendrie, A., *The Cinderella Service: RAF Coastal Command, 1939–1945* (Pen & Sword, 2006).

Henshaw, A., *Sigh for a Merlin* (Blackett, 1977; reprinted by Crecy Publishing Ltd, 2007).

'Hurricane Special', *The Aeroplane*, October 2007.

Jackson, A.J., *Blackburn Aircraft since 1909* (Putnam, 1968).

James, D.N., *Gloster Aircraft since 1917* (Putnam, 1971).

James, D.N., *Schneider Trophy Aircraft, 1913–1931* (Putnam, 1981).

Jane's All the World's Aircraft: 1921–1937 (Sampson Low).

Killen, J., *A History of Marine Aviation* (Muller, 1969).

King, H.F., *Aeromarine Origins* (Putnam, 1966).

Lewis, J., *Racing Ace: the Fights and Flights of 'Kink' Kinkead* (Pen & Sword, 2011).

Livock, G.E., *To the Ends of the Air* (HMSO, 1973).

London, P., *Saunders and Saro Aircraft since 1917* (Putnam, 1974).

McKinstry, L., *Spitfire: Portrait of a Legend* (Murray, 2007).

Mason, F.K., *Saunders Aircraft since 1920* (Putnam, 1961).

Mason, T., *British Flight Testing: Martlesham Heath, 1920–1939* (Putney, 1993).

Meekoms, K.J., and E.B. Morgan, *The British Aircraft Specifications File, 1920–1949* (Air Britain, 1994).

Mitchell, Dr Gordon (Ed.), *R.J. Mitchell – Schooldays to Spitfire* (Nelson & Saunders, 1986; reprinted by Tempus Publishing, 2006).

Mitchell, R.J., 'Racing Seaplanes and their Influence on Design', Aeronautical Engineering Supplement to *The Aeroplane*, 25 December, 1929.

Mitchell, RJ., 'Schneider Trophy Machine Design, 1927', Proceedings of the 3rd meeting, 63rd session of the Royal Aeronautical Society.

Mondey, D., *The Schneider Trophy* (R. Hale, 1975).

Morgan, E.B., and E. Shacklady, *Spitfire: The History* (Kay Publishing, 1987).

Munson, K., *Flying Boats and Seaplanes since 1910* (Macmillan, 1971).

Nicholl, G.W.R., *The Supermarine Walrus; the Story of a Unique Aircraft* (G.T. Foulis & Co., 1966).

Orlebar, Wing Commander A.H., *The Schneider Trophy* (AFC Seeley Service and Co., 1933).

'P.BP 31E Nighthawk', *The Aviation Historian*, Issue No. 8.

Pegram, R., *The Schneider Trophy Seaplanes and Flying Boats: Victors, Vanquished and Visions* (Fonthill Media, 2012).

Penny, R.E., 'Seaplane Development' (with contribution by R.J. Mitchell), *Journal of the Royal Aeronautical Society*, September 1927.

Penrose, H., *British Aviation: the Great War and Armistice: 1915–1919* (Putnam, 1969).

Penrose, H., *British Aviation: the Adventuring Years: 1920–1929* (Putnam, 1973).

Penrose, H., *British Aviation: Widening Horizons: 1930–1934* (Putnam, 1979).

Price, A., *The Spitfire Story* (Jane's, 1982).

Pudney, J., *A Pride of Unicorns: Richard and David Atcherley of the RAF* (Oldbourne Book Co. Ltd, 1960).

Quill, J., *Spitfire: a Test Pilot's Story* (Murray, 1983; reprinted by Crecy Publishing Ltd, 1998).

Rendall, I., *Spitfire; Icon of a Nation* (Orion Publishing Group, 2009).

Robertson, B., *Spitfire; the Story of a Famous Fighter* (Harleyford, 1960).

Russell, C.R., *Spitfire Odyssey* (Kingfisher Railway Productions, 1985).

Schofield, Flight Lieutenant H.M., *The High Speed and Other Flights* (John Hamilton Ltd, 1932).

Scott, J.D., *Vickers: A History* (Weidenfeld & Nicholson, 1962).

Shelton, J.K., *Schneider Trophy to Spitfire; the Design Career of R.J. Mitchell* (Haynes, 2008).

Shenstone, B.S., 'Transport Flying-Boats: Life and Death', *Journal of the Royal Aeronautical Society*, December, 1969.

Sinnot, C., *The Royal Air Force and Aircraft Design, 1923–1939* (Frank Cass, 2001).

Smith, J., 'The First Mitchell Memorial Lecture', *Journal of the Royal Aeronautical Society*, 58, 1954.

Smith, J., 'R.J. Mitchell, Aircraft Designer', *The Aeroplane*, 29 January 1954.

Snaith, Group Captain L.C., 'Schneider Trophy Flying', 1968 Lecture to the Royal Aeronautical Society Historical Group.

Spitfire 70 – A FlyPast Special (Key Publishing, 2006).

'The Supermarine Walrus and Seagull Variants', Profile No. 224, *Profile Publications*.

Taylor, H.A., *Fairey Aircraft since 1915* (Putnam, 1974).

Templewood, Viscount (Sir Samuel Hoare), *Empire of the Air: The Advent of the Air Age, 1922–1929* (Collins, 1957).

Waghorn, Flight Lieutenant R.D.H, 'The Schneider Trophy, 1929', *Royal Aeronautical Society*, May 1930 (Yeovil Branch).

Webb, Denis Le P., *Never a Dull Moment at Supermarine: A Personal History* (J&KH Publishing, 2001).

INDEX

Also from The History Press

WAR IN
THE SKIES

Find these titles and more at
www.thehistorypress.co.uk